Stress-Proof Your Body

**Release your tension, boost your energy and feel
fantastic every day**

PAUL CHAPMAN

D1319027

Published by Fairwater Press, Reading, England

Email: publisher@fairwaterpress.com

First published by Fairwater Press in 2013

ISBN: 978-0-9927081-0-8

CONTENTS

ACKNOWLEDGEMENTS

Books don't write themselves, and my thanks go to my wife Amreeta for her endless patience, my editor Jane Hammett, my cover designer Emily Moran and my two children Shikana and Devlin, without whose input this book would have been written in half the time!

Preface

For over thirty-five years now I have been studying the little-known Jade Dragon system of tai chi and kung fu. This school comes originally from the Jade Dragon mountain in South West China. The skills are based on the philosophy of Daoism - one of the three main philosophical schools of China alongside Buddhism and Confucianism.

Many Daoist schools of old taught advanced martial arts (kung fu) skills to strengthen the physical structure, release unneeded tensions and to help understand the effects that different forces have on the mind and body. The kung fu skills that were developed in this school became known as the Jade Dragon system. In 2003 I set up the Jade Dragon kung fu school in England, which I have run ever since.

Kung fu has a huge range of principles and practices to develop the human body, mind and spirit and to enable the follower to live a life in harmony with himself and the world around him. It's not so much about fighting others as fighting yourself – your fears, tensions, poor habits and so on.

This is my first book and is the first in a series of books aimed to give the reader a series of practices for healthy living. Each book will investigate the issue from a Chinese perspective and will give a series of principles and exercises to help you develop yourself fully.

The first two books will focus on what both Chinese and Westerners will recognise as perhaps the biggest threat to human health and wellbeing – stress. This book focuses on the physical aspect of stress, which is accumulated tension, whereas the second book will focus on the mental and emotional aspects of stress. To the Chinese, excess physical tension imprisons the body and a lack of mental focus and emotional control interferes with the fulfilling of one's destiny. Future books will focus on developing and building your energy. However, the two main reasons why many people are unable to feel their energy is due to too many blockages in the form of tension and a lack of mental focus.

Few people outside the Far East are aware of the huge range of exercises and skills that have been developed over thousands of years by the Chinese apart, perhaps, from taijiquan (tai chi chuan). The monks of antiquity developed deep philosophies and phenomenally powerful exercises to rid the body of tensions and the mind of its idle chattering and often destructive thoughts. The body and mind could then work together as a perfect team to develop extraordinary abilities and fulfil its potential, to help them understand themselves and their place in the natural order of things.

I hope you will enjoy this book and will gain as much benefit from it as I have gained from writing it.

Introduction

Stress is everywhere; it's unavoidable. The speed of change in the world today is frightening and, as stress is often caused by change, then I think it's true to say that mankind has never lived in more stressful times.

Some people seem to be very good at dealing with stress. They can cope, even thrive, in highly stressful situations. Other people seem to fall apart at the slightest pressure. My aim in this book is to help you become one of those people who can remain relatively unaffected by stressful situations and so can stay in control of yourself and the situations you may find yourself in.

This book will help you make some fundamental changes to the way you respond to stress. It aims to help you release some of the tension that you habitually hold on to, to give you more energy and generally to make you a more efficient version of yourself, one who is far better able to cope with the stresses of life. The central message of this book is that you cannot avoid stress – but you can change the ways in which you react to it. This book details various principles and practices that will help you change your reactions to stress and, in so doing, help you become calmer, more balanced and with the resources to cope with whatever life throws your way.

The knowledge in this book comes largely from the philosophy of Daoism and from the Chinese art of kung fu. Much more than just a fighting art, kung fu is a complete system of human development and understanding. One of the major aims of kung fu is to develop the 'kung fu body'. That is a body that is free of unnecessary tension, which is light, mobile, powerful and able to withstand physical and emotional pressure. The 'kung fu body' is designed to last the whole of your life and should not start to wear out when you're just in your fifties or sixties. Through kung fu and tai chi training we come to understand that life always contains conflict but that we should strive to find balance within that conflict. The conflicts that go on in our lives often become mirrored by internal conflict, which leads to a build-up of long-term tension. Finding a balance inside us helps us to release that tension. It also helps us to understand and balance the external factors that are going on in

1

our lives, which will in turn enable us to live a happier, more productive and healthier existence.

The main areas we will be looking at to help you deal with stress and tension are:

Internal expansion – learning to release contraction by expanding.

Natural breathing – using your breathing to release tension and give you more energy.

Posture and movement – changing the way you sit, stand and move in ways that no longer hold on to tensions and that allow you to relax.

Flexibility – stretching principles to make your body feel lighter, free of constriction and to help it move with fluid grace.

A *lighter touch* – learning how to interact with your world with more efficiency and intelligence.

Stress can cause you to develop a huge number of physical, mental and emotional ills. Note that stress doesn't *cause* them, but it can cause you to *develop* them. It's a subtle but important difference. The effects of stress aren't inevitable. You can change how you cope with stress. You can also release many of the effects that stress has caused to build up in you ever since you were a young child. You can feel freer, have more energy, feel stronger in yourself and learn not to fear change but to embrace it.

This book is partially about stress but it is more about tension, and it's important to understand the difference. 'Stress' means the bad things that happen to you – the arguments with your partner, the extra work your boss is forcing you to do, the endless sets of red traffic lights on your way home, and so on. 'Stressed' is how you feel when you're being pushed in a direction you don't want to go or when demands are being made of you that you don't feel you have the resources to cope with.

When you feel stressed, your body reacts physically by generating tension.

Tension is how you react to stress and that tension lasts a lot longer than the stressful situation that triggered it; in fact, in some cases it can last the rest of your life! So, to be clear, even if you don't feel that you're a stressed person, you are almost certainly a tense one. If you weren't a tense person you would have the flexibility of a young child. If you don't, then this book is for you.

Stress and tension are two very different things: you can be stressed without tensing up (this is very rare and usually requires the kind of training this book gives you) and, equally, you can be very tense without feeling at all stressed. This is very common, to be tense without feeling stressed. Each chapter of this book will help you to understand your tension, find out where it is, and give you a set of practices and principles to get rid of it.

Only by reducing your tension load can you increase your ability to cope with stress effectively.

One of the key messages this book has is that, in order to change your life for the better, you need to become more self-aware. That means you need to become more aware of how you are standing, how you are breathing, and so on, and to feel how these things change when you are stressed or tired, angry or depressed. Virtually every move you make is, at least partially, habitual. The way you hold your arms when you drive, how you place your feet when you walk, how you sit at your computer, are all habits that you have developed over time and you no longer need to think about them. Unfortunately, they aren't necessarily the best way to do things, so this book will help you to get rid of some of your deepest habits and exchange them for more efficient and healthier ways of doing things.

The mind–body mirror

The first thing you need to understand is the mind–body connection, or what I call the mirror. What this means is that what happens in the body is reflected in the mind, and vice versa. This connection is extremely powerful and research shows that our bodies are the physical expressions of our mind and, equally, our minds are the mental expression of our bodies. What happens in either the body or the mind will affect both.

A good example of this is the placebo effect which, as we all know, enables a person to improve their physical health just because they believe they have taken a powerful medicine. The more powerful the medicine is supposed to be, the stronger the placebo effect becomes. The mind creates the physical effects in the body that the powerful medicine was supposed to create. Another good example is the way in which your posture reflects your mood. If you are happy and excited your posture will be radically different than if you are depressed.

Let's take a quick look at the road ahead.

Chapter 1 defines stress – what it is and its effects. We will see how the lack of balance in our lives pushes us mentally one way and another and pits muscle against muscle, leading to long-term tension and its associated problems. We can see and feel how exhausting this is both physically and mentally. We take a look at the three different ways we react to stress and their effects. The chapter also takes us on a brief trip back in time to see where our typical reactions to stress come from and show how modern life is both far safer and yet far more stressful than the lives of our ancestors.

Chapter 2 puts tension under the microscope. It examines the reasons why tensing your muscles when you feel stressed is a natural and habitual act. Yet, despite this, it is an act that eventually prompts most visits to the doctor, wears you out physically and mentally, and shortens your useful life span. It shows clearly that it isn't stress that is the problem, but the tension that comes from stress. It talks about theories of why people hold on to so much tension.

This chapter also demonstrates why some people can handle highly stressful situations with ease, while others fall apart at the slightest pressure. It shows how and why you get tense, and why it is so difficult for you to relax. We look at the common methods people use to relax and see how and why they fail to reduce our general levels of tension. All of these work to some degree, but the effects are usually short-term and some of them have nasty side-effects. Most importantly, this chapter discusses the tension paradox, which makes it virtually impossible for you or anyone else to relax properly.

Chapter 3 discusses and explains the expansion principle. This gives an answer to the tension paradox. Finally: a working, long-term answer to tension. It gives exercises to release specific tensions as well as a general tension-reliever. These are based on a new principle called the expansion principle, and can produce more powerful results than traditional exercises such as progressive muscle relaxation.

Chapter 4 discusses the importance of good breathing, which cannot be overstated. It lists the vast panoply of benefits that improved breathing will bring to your life – as well as the dismayingly long list of illnesses to which poor breathing has been linked. It looks at some simple changes you can make to your breathing habits that will give you more energy and help you to relax. Balanced breathing leads gradually to balance in mind and body. Again the expansion principle comes into full effect here. This is far too powerful to ignore. As an added bonus, the chapter includes a cure for hiccups that actually works!

Chapter 5 is all about your inability to maintain a healthy posture. From the moment you leave the womb, all your tensions are stored in and are echoed in your posture. Your posture, therefore, is a map of your life and defines and reflects your lifestyle, identity, current mood and state of mind and health. Unfortunately, most people have severe patterns of tension that distort their posture and put great strain on various physical and mental processes. You can begin to see how locked up you are and find a way to unlocking yourself and opening up from the inside. We examine the common postural problems suffered by many people, along with information on how they damage your body and mind.

Chapter 6 teaches you the keys to a good posture. A good posture is one that is aligned with the forces acting on it and holds on to only as much tension as is necessary to maintain those forces in balance. When the forces are allowed to flow through relaxed muscles and are then diverted into the ground, all kinds of physical and mental pressures/stresses can be withstood with relative equanimity.

To obtain a stress-proof posture, four things need to occur. This chapter goes into those four requisites in detail, showing you how you can dramatically improve your health and the way you feel about yourself simply by changing the way you hold yourself.

Chapter 7 discusses movement. Gaining a good posture is the first step, but you need to be able to maintain those principles while moving. Luckily, this chapter is full of tips and tricks to help you walk, run and move without developing too much excess tension.

Chapter 8 is all about flexibility. A flexible body is one that has minimum tensions and so is able to cope with stresses with far greater ease. Being more flexible makes you feel great and improves your posture and makes all movement easier. Through stretching exercises, you can find out where you are holding on to tension generally, and also how tense you become during your day. You will find out how your body should feel when your joints are more open and mobile, and your muscles and other soft tissues have learned to let go.

This chapter helps you to develop a personal stretching programme that makes use of the expansion principle plus the principles of posture to help you develop a more flexible body quickly and safely. It explains why core strength is so important in gaining flexibility, and also covers the use of the mind and breathing when stretching. This chapter also introduces a new method of doing stretching exercises which makes use of Daoist principles of aligning yourself with the forces acting on you. Around 90% of my students have found that their flexibility improves in one session when they try out this method.

Chapter 9 examines the impact you have on the world – and it has on you – through your sense of touch. All too often, your internal imbalances mean that your connections with the people and environment around you are clumsy and ineffectual, which leads to further, unnecessary stress. The more control you have over yourself, the more control you will have over your influence on the world around you. In this chapter you will learn the 'LIGHTER touch'. This is a powerful principle that increases your sensitivity, power and grace. No longer will your movements be clumsy, forceful or insensitive. You will learn how to keep your mind in your body and react better to every situation.

You will also learn how to be sensitive to your personal space and that of others. You will learn not to allow another person's invasion of your personal space to affect you. This alone will prevent many tensions from building up inside you. Finally, this chapter will show you how to feel at home wherever you are and be more comfortable in any situation.

Chapter 10 says that happiness is not dependent on anything, but should be your default state. Tensions arising from negative life events may temporarily drain you of energy and happiness. It is much easier to be happy when you are full of energy and balanced inside. With your improved posture, good breathing habits and increased knowledge of how to stay relaxed in the face of pressure, unconditional happiness is much easier to attain and maintain. This chapter includes ten steps towards happiness and tells you how to improve your happiness with each step. It gives an explanation of what misery is, should you find yourself being pushed towards your old ways of thinking and being, and finally includes one of the best exercises in the book – the whole-body smile.

This book contains a lot of knowledge, theories, principles and practices. Don't expect to be able to master everything in this book in one sitting. There are too many things to focus on. A good approach would be to try each of the exercises several times and then see which ones work best for you. As everything in your body is connected, a reduction in tension anywhere in your system will lead to a reduction in tension everywhere else. Once you have found some practices that work for you, then do them regularly and make them a part of your life. When these have been 'hardwired' into your life and your body then you can experiment with other practices. Gaining a good understanding of the theories and principles in this book will enable you to adapt the practices here to suit you and your life. Do not take this book, or any other, as dogma or gospel. You are a unique individual, so feel free to adapt these exercises accordingly. Over time you should return to this book and you will find new knowledge contained within it. Different aspects of it will make sense to you as your practice develops. You will find that the methods used here will relate directly to many other physical, internal or spiritual practices that you may engage in.

This book offers both a journey and a system. Along your journey there are several stopping-off points where you can examine the ways in which you have failed to maintain balance and harmony in your life and, in doing so, allowed tension to take over your body, mind and emotions.

The more balanced you are internally, the less tension you will hold on to.

The definition of balance is a system that is held in perfect equilibrium. Most human beings fall far short of balance, and so become victims of conflicting tensions, uncontrolled emotions and fluctuating energy levels.

Everybody is different. Some people fall apart at the first sign of stress. They have little tolerance for change and little belief in their own resources to cope. However, some people manage to remain fairly neutral in the way they deal with stress. They seem to have more control, they deal with stressful situations more appropriately and, as a result, they are more respected because of it. This is because they don't become locked up with tension when faced with pressure. This book aims to help you become more like them by changing the way you do some fundamental things. It will take you on a journey from being stressed, unhealthy and unhappy to having more control over yourself, your life, your relationships, and your levels of energy and stress.

Wouldn't it be wonderful if everyone could control their stress simply by changing their breathing patterns, and also could use their posture to prevent the negative effects of tension from building up inside them? If they could, the world would be a far happier, healthier and more peaceful place.

CHAPTER 1

The Stress of Change

In this chapter

> What is stress and why do I have it?
>
> What are the three ways I react to stress, and what does my default strategy tell me about myself?
>
> Why do you say that reducing the stress I'm under is not the best way to deal with my physical and emotional health?

Stress seems to be a word that is on everybody's lips at the moment. It's a word that crops up in all subjects from health to economics to celebrities. But just what is it and, crucially, why does it affect some people so much more than others?

This chapter will help you define what stress is, then will go on to look at the main ways in which people respond to stress. It will provide some background in the form of a very brief history of stress and finally will ask what, if anything, modern medicine can do to help you deal with stress.

What is stress?

Stress has been defined as:

> 'a state of mental or emotional strain or tension resulting from adverse or demanding circumstances' (Oxford English Dictionary)

> 'stress, in psychology and biology, any environmental or physical pressure that elicits a response from an organism. In most cases, stress promotes survival because it forces organisms to adapt to rapidly changing environmental conditions. However, when an organism's response to stress is inadequate or when the stress is too powerful, disease or death of an organism may result' (Encyclopaedia Britannica)

In my opinion, the top definition by the OED has it wrong. It is confusing stress with tension. It's important to know the difference, so we will cover that shortly. Encyclopaedia Britannica says it best. It clarifies that stress is any kind of pressure that elicits a response from an organism, particularly where the pressure is such that the organism may not have the resources to cope with it.

There is no universally recognised definition of stress; however, we all know what it is. It is the demands made upon an organism, i.e. you, which you feel you don't have the resources to cope with. This sends alarm bells ringing in your brain and triggers defence mechanisms throughout your body. These vary depending on the nature and severity of the perceived 'threat', but will include at least some of the following: increased heart rate, raised blood pressure, and a partial shutdown of non-essential processes such as food digestion (leading to stomach problems, irritable bowel syndrome (IBS) etc.), decreased sex drive and TENSION (this is in capitals for a reason!).

All of these are aimed at preparing the body for fight or flight by diverting extra blood to the muscles and shutting down non-essential processes.

A word that is synonymous with stress is pressure. I often feel that stress is just like being pushed, or pressured, in a direction in which you don't want to go. Clearly, if you wanted to go in that direction then it wouldn't be stressful. Imagine for a moment that happening to you. It's bad enough being pushed forward where you can see the situation you are being forced into. For many people, what is worse is the feeling of being pushed backwards into the unknown.

Fear of the unknown or fear of change is one of the primary causes of stress. I'm sure many more people would happily change jobs or relationships if they knew in advance what they were getting into. It's the not knowing that forces people to stay in unsuitable jobs or failing relationships long after they should get out.

The three responses to stress
Imagine you were being pressured into a situation that you weren't happy with. There would be three possible reactions to this:

1. Give in to the pressure.

2. Push back.

3. Escape from it or avoid it somehow.

These have been your three options for dealing with all the stress you have had in your life to date. The kind of person you are now has been – to a great extent – dictated by which of the three has been your preferred option. We all use all three to a degree, but one of these will dominate. This dominant option would have been set early in your childhood and would have been the one that got you what you wanted most reliably. None of these are intrinsically any better than the others, as each has its advantages and disadvantages.

Option 1 – to give in

Some things you just can't fight against and, recognising that to be the case, we just give in. However, we will never give in entirely – our egos will never accept that we are completely helpless, so there is usually a contraction deep inside us that represents not so much an attempt to resist the situation but an armouring of our deepest selves to protect us from feelings of helplessness and the consequences of what we may be giving ourselves up to.

If your default mode is to give in to pressure, then you tend not to cope well with pressure. You just want an easy life and tend to be risk-averse. You will probably live long, but it's unlikely you will prosper. The prosperous are those who are prepared to take big risks and can deal with the associated pressures over the long term.

Option 2 – to push back

The act of being pushed around will cause certain muscles to tense up to physically oppose the push. However, most of the pressures we face in life aren't physical, so can't be physically opposed. If your boss dumps a load of extra work on you towards the end of the day that must be finished before you go home you can't physically push it back in his or her face – no matter how much you may want to. However, certain muscles will tense up in resistance to the fact you are being forced to take on more work.

11

If there was something to physically push against then, when the force was removed, those muscles of yours that opposed it could relax again. However, in a case like this there is no physical pressure so your muscles stay tensed, possibly for a long time – usually much longer than the mental tension that caused the muscles to contract in the first place.

This tension, which is largely subconscious, adds to the many other layers of tension that already exist and which are forming an armour of tension that covers much of your body.

If you are the pushing back type, then you will probably get more of what you want than those opting for option 1. But the downside is that you are likely to be highly stressed. Those who push their way through life may well become powerful people, this if often gained at a price; through fear. Without the ability to respect others and to compromise, your life will lack harmony and this will be reflected in your own health and destiny.

Option 3 – evade the pressure

This, of course, is the healthiest option and we get a lot of self-satisfaction from the feeling of having 'got one over the system'. We usually get a sudden buzz of energy when we work out a way around a stressful situation, and this 'buzz' comes largely from the sudden release of tension in the muscles and the energy that's no longer tied up in holding on to all that tension. Those who prefer this option are clever, resourceful people who use their brains to get them out of trouble. This can be a good thing, but sometimes they may fail to see the bigger picture and end up dumping the pressure on someone else then congratulate themselves for having avoided the stressful situation.

Think about times when you have felt threatened or stressed. Can you identify which of these is your default strategy? In the long term, the tactics you use to deal with stress will define your personality. If you are the 'push back' type of person, you may become an aggressive, angry person, possibly a control freak whom many people will find hard to deal with. If, on the other hand, you are the 'collapse and give in' type, then you could become a passive doormat for others, probably prone to depression, with the feeling that every time you try to get up there is someone ready to push you down again. Obviously these are extremes, and most people will fit somewhere in between.

Stress is almost always caused by change.

Clearly, if a situation never changes then it can't be stressful, as you know precisely what to expect, although monotony itself can be a cause of stress. It's when things change that stress occurs, as you often don't know what it's going to change into and if you are going to be able to cope with it. The less you know about what it's changing into and the greater potential effect that could have on your life, then the greater the stress is. The common most stressful situations such as moving house, divorce, death, changing job, and so on, all change your life dramatically and you can't see exactly how your life will be afterwards. Fear of change is a powerful thing and it keeps many people locked into bad jobs or disastrous relationships because they fear the alternative, or perhaps can't even see an alternative. All they can see is frying pans and fires and so they hesitate to jump.

Smaller stressful situations happen to us all every single day. Much of traditional stress management training focuses on reducing the stresses in your working day, which often put people under enormous pressure. However, your home, family and social life can also be highly stressful so, rather than focusing on reducing some of your stresses, it is more effective to change the way that you, personally, cope with stress.

A brief history of stress: from grunting to Googling

Life has never been so easy but conversely it has also never been so stressful. How did we all come to be so stressed, contracted and cut off from ourselves and the world around us? It hasn't always been this way.

In pre-industrial societies, life moved at a walking pace and changed with the seasons. There was no pressure to get things done by 5pm; the pace of life was much slower. Many more people than now lived in small villages and so they knew their neighbours and friends very well. They opened their hearts and arms to each other with little of the distrust and protective layering that we instinctively use on meeting other people today. Most people also tended to live around others of the same social class, and the ferocious competition for material advantage we all take part in today simply didn't exist back then except among the higher classes. Obviously, people worried about ill-health, poverty and deprivation, but generally people lived closer to nature, emotionally closer to each other and didn't suffer from the stress-related conditions common in today's society.

Then along came the industrial revolution and with it came a huge change in working practices, production targets, bosses, working conditions and so on. Life started to become stressful as the production of goods had to keep up with demand. Many people moved out of their villages and into towns to work in the new factories. The towns grew larger and became cities. However, the living and working conditions were terrible, with most people living in small, cramped houses with shared toilets, open sewers and no clean water. Children weren't educated and were expected to work for their living from a very young age, often in appalling conditions.

When times are hard, most animals instinctively retreat into themselves for protection. Hedgehogs roll themselves into a prickly ball; tortoises and snails retreat into their shells. We have no external armour to protect us, so we subconsciously armour ourselves with layers of physical tension, contracting the muscles around areas of pain to form a protective shield. Also, when things are tough, then people tend to lose their respect for each other and anger, blame and resentment fester. It is very hard to open up to another person if you expect that person to be critical and judgemental, and so we close ourselves off from real communication with all but a select few of our friends.

Over the last two hundred years, life has been getting faster and faster and the speed of change is now increasing at a prodigious rate. Change is happening all around us. It is relentless, and is constantly being pushed in our face by the plethora of machines we have available to tell us all the bad things that are happening everywhere in the world, whether they relate to us or not, whether we can do anything about them or not.

> *"Life is a series of natural and spontaneous changes. Don't resist them--that only creates sorrow."*
> — Lao Tzu, Dao De Jing (Tao Te Ching)

We now live in a world that is no longer run by politicians but by the media, who have the power to make or break anyone or anything. The media, knowing that bad news sells, report and exaggerate items that will increase the stress levels of their readership. This constant barrage of bad news is coupled with advertisements telling us what we should be wearing or doing, what we should look like and how we should live; and it all makes us feel that we aren't living the life we could – and perhaps should – be living.

So we contract further into ourselves, recognising that we feel stressed but not fully realising why. Our bodies close up and become rigid with tension which interferes with many of our natural processes; our minds clog up with worries, guilt, fears and insecurities about our lives, and we have nobody to turn to for help as we are too closed off from communicating our weaknesses to others. So we turn to professional therapists who, unlike most of us, are trained to listen to our stresses and offer sound advice to help us realise we aren't alone, we aren't weird, and also help us to understand why we are feeling what we are feeling.

> Is there an answer to this? Yes, indeed. That's what this book is for.
>
> Is it simple, quick and pain-free? I'm afraid not.
>
> But is it worth it? Definitely. Read on to find out more.

When you are under stress, tension develops in your body. There are many reasons and theories for why this is so, which I will cover in the next chapter. However, the important thing to remember is that it is this tension that causes the physical effects of stress, and that *only by reducing the tensions you're holding on to can you learn to cope more easily with stressful situations.*

This book makes no claims about helping to reduce the stresses you are coping with and the pressures you're under. There are Stress Management courses and books aplenty to help you identify and learn to reduce the situations that cause you stress. However, people are going on Stress Management courses, managing their time, becoming more assertive, learning to say no, sharing their feelings and so on and yet they still feel stressed and still suffer from the physical and mental ills associated with it.

The main problem with this approach is that you can never control all the stresses you face in life. You may be able to manage your workload more efficiently, but then you may have a stressful home life.

This book takes a different approach and teaches you to change how you react when you are under pressure. Your stressful situations may remain, but you will have more tools to manage that stress with far greater ease. In fact, you will change to become a person who no longer holds on to stress in the same way, and thus is healthier and happier in so many different ways.

A summary of Chapter 1

Stress is here to stay. Modern life is one of endless change and constant pressure. If you are going to be able to deal with it with your health and sanity intact, then you too must learn to change and adapt.

You must learn to take responsibility for your own health. This book will give you a range of ways to better understand yourself and how you react to stress. It will point to changes you can make to help you cope with the pressures in your life.

Some of these changes are simple, others less so, but all of them are profound when practised often.

Good luck.

CHAPTER 2

The Tension Paradox

In this chapter

> How can my tension levels be responsible for such a huge range of my physical and mental ills?
>
> If becoming tense is so bad for me, then why do I do it?
>
> I'm told that I need to relax but I've tried everything and nothing seems to relax me. Why is it so hard to relax?
>
> I'm in pain but I don't want to rely on pain medication. Is my tension contributing to the pain I'm in, or even causing it? What can I do to alleviate my pain without drugs?

This is perhaps the most important chapter in this book. It examines muscular tension and explains why excess tension is so dangerous, why we develop tension when under stress, and why it is so difficult to let go of. We will look at the common methods people use to relax and see why they may not offer any long-term stress relief.

At the heart of this chapter is an understanding of the tension paradox. This is probably the most important concept in the book as it clearly explains why tension is such a problem and why no effective solutions have yet been found (and won't be found until people start recognising that it is tension that is the culprit and not stress).

We will examine the major role that tension plays in most pain and injuries and see how reducing your tension will give you back the body you were born to have – one that is fluid, expressive and adaptable to its environment – in other words, one that can cope with and adapt to the constant changes of life in the twenty-first century. We will include one quick exercise that can get rid of a lot of the tension in your shoulders in just a couple of minutes.

It often seems to me that high levels of tension can make a person appear brittle. The slightest, smallest amount of extra pressure can break them. In fact the definition of brittle is that of a material that is excessively stiff and liable to break easily when under pressure. Some people are so rigid with tension that they can barely move and this has huge effects on their ability to handle stress, their general health or lack of it and on their attitudes to life. Rigidity in the body is mirrored by rigidity in the mind. My aim is to soften your tension and so allow you to bend, to become more flexible in the way you deal with stressful situations. When pressure comes you align yourself with it, learn to adapt yourself to it and so are able to survive it more easily.

Trees that don't bend with the wind won't last the storm.
(Old Chinese proverb)

The painful, debilitating, imprisoning effects of tension

This book is about helping you to develop a stress-proof body. The central message is that the more tension you are holding on to, then the more you will suffer when faced with stressful situations. Release your tension and stress becomes much easier to handle.

The tension that stress creates is literally killing you slowly. Reduce your tension load and you will gain more useful years in your life. You may die at the same age, but the years leading up to your death won't be so plagued with ill-health and limited mobility. Let us look at the effects that excess tension has on us and our lives. Everything you have heard in the past relating to stress is actually caused by the tension you develop due to stressful situations you have coped with in the past. Remember, the stress may only last for a few minutes or hours, but the tension that comes from it can remain for the rest of your life.

It is estimated that anywhere between 60–90% of visits to
the doctor are stress/tension related.

The physical effects of tension are wide and varied and include, but are not limited to, the following.

Raised blood pressure and heart rate

This comes from the increased needs of the muscles during periods of stress. The heart pumps out more blood to feed the fight or flight reflex. However, the increased blood flow is restricted by muscular tension, so blood pressure rises. This puts great strain on your heart which has to work harder than it should to meet the oxygen needs of the body's systems.

Pain including headaches migraine, back pain, etc.

Most chronic pain (which doesn't stem from a recent injury) is related to tension. Tight muscles pull on certain areas of the body and so other muscles have to pull back to maintain the structure. This tug of war gradually intensifies and spreads until certain muscles can take no more and send pain messages to the brain. Often, the actual source of the pain isn't at the site of pain at all. For example, pain in the chest often stems from excess tension in the neck muscles.

Poor sleep patterns

This stems from an inability to stop thinking and rethinking all the day's issues. Added to this is the physical tension which prevents the body from relaxing and letting go enough to trigger true sleep.

Low energy/increased fatigue

Holding on to tension continuously, day after day, year after year, is a draining process. It's one of the main reasons why children have so much more energy than their parents. Children haven't yet developed much tension, and so they have far more energy available to them and a constant curiosity about testing their own physical limits. For adults, however, carrying a lot of tension around is like walking around all day with a heavy rucksack on your back.

Clenching jaw/grinding teeth

It is often the case that you might want to speak or shout out against a stressful situation that you're in, but can't. So you subconsciously clamp your teeth together to prevent it. This can easily turn into a long-standing habitual reaction to stress. It leads to headaches, dental problems and eventually TMJD (temporomandibular joint disorder) which can cause a horrifying panoply of symptoms.

Digestive disorders including constipation and IBS
This comes from the large amounts of tension we hold in the waist and hip area, which prevents proper digestion of food due to the constriction of the digestive organs.

Arthritis
The tension in your muscles is constantly pulling on your joints. This can cause excess wear on the joints and lead to osteoarthritis.

Sexual disorders such as infertility, erectile dysfunction and impotence
Again, due to constriction of the vital organs and reduction in the blood supply to them.

Cold hands and feet in the winter – poor circulation
Tension restricts blood flow down the arms and legs, and less blood getting to the hands and feet makes them feel cold.

Excess physical tension also leads to mental and emotional issues, since what happens in the body is mirrored in the mind. I will deal with these in detail in my next book: *Stress Proof Your Mind*. Briefly, these issues include depression, mental fatigue, forgetfulness, negative thinking, low self-esteem, anger issues, anxiety/panic attacks and many other issues.

If tension is so debilitating, why do we have it?

> *'I take thee to be my awful, dreaded tension. To have and to hold, from this day forward, for better, for worse, for richer, for poorer, till death us do part. And hereto I give thee my energy.'*

From the cradle to the grave, we spend our lives accumulating tensions. We aren't born with them; therefore, they aren't our birthright. Children, free from the clutching straitjackets of tension, are free to move with boundless joy and energy. They are loose and flexible of limb and are similarly unconfined in their thinking.

Unfortunately, we've all seen the other end of the scale: elderly people near the end of their lives who are physically imprisoned by the tension in their own bodies. These tensions can cause severe, unremitting pain coupled with a huge loss of mobility, which can cause problems with walking, standing, bending and all manner of other movements. It also drains their bodies of strength, grace and balance.

This lack of physical flexibility mirrors their lack of mental flexibility. This isn't always the case, but I'm sure we all know elderly people who have limited thinking patterns, their values seem outdated and so, unable to accept change, they spend much of their time and precious energy complaining about the world today. Our care homes are full of people whose physical tensions are so extreme that they're plain for all to see – the dowager's humps, barely movable hips and legs, distorted shoulders, heads constantly thrust forward and down, etc.

Incidentally, if you want to see distorted posture, you don't need to look just at the elderly. Look around at almost any adult (or even try looking in the mirror) and you will see distorted postures caused by a variety of tension patterns. Very few bodies are symmetrical. Most people have one shoulder higher than the other, or hips out of alignment, or their head tilted to one side. Many people believe that gradual physical deterioration is inevitable, but is it really? Yes, our bodies do get old and deteriorate, but we can slow down that process dramatically by following a few simple principles and practices.

One of the reasons that prompted me to write this book is that, as I look around me, I see the situation getting worse. The postural abnormalities that used to be seen only in the over-40s are now increasingly common in people in their 20s. I believe this is largely due to the fixed positions that we spend most of our days in – computers, cars and sofas being the main culprits. People generally move less than they did 20 years ago. More people are sedentary in offices, children don't play outside any more but sit inside in front of a TV, computer or games console. Another key reason is the high levels of stress that so many people are under, which contracts the body and withers the soul.

The physical tension that comes from these fixed positions and high stress levels builds up gradually over months and years, and huge amounts of our resources are consumed in holding on to all that tension. The body is slowly throttled to death from the inside out and we end our days stiff of limb, brittle of bone and unclear of mind. This book will help you learn to undo this damage, and my aim is for you to add years to your life as well as adding life to your years. Can you believe that in your 80s you could possibly be fitter and healthier than you are today? If you regularly follow the principles outlined in this text, you stand a good chance of being fit and healthy well into your old age.

Why does stress cause tension to develop?

When the body or mind is put under stress, the muscles tense up. Here are the main theories behind why this happens.

Tension in the muscles physically armours the body from attack. This theory is borne out by the fact that one of the first places we become tense is in the abdominal area. Tensing this area clearly protects the digestive and reproductive organs from damage.

Tension stabilises the body against change. Change can be very frightening for many people, particularly if they have no control over it. They can feel like a cork bobbing on the ocean at the mercy of every passing current. Tensing the muscles gives at least some feeling of stability. The principles discussed later in this book – of expansion, postural rooting, internal connection and whole-body breathing – will give you a core feeling of power that will enable you to handle change in your life with equanimity.

Tension prevents expression. The modern age allows few routes for self-expression. It is not appropriate to shout, scream, dance with joy or burst into tears just because you feel like it. Your emotions want to be let out, they want full rein, but 'civilised' people don't do that, so we learn that we can control these errant emotions by tensing up in the right places.

The subconscious fighting back. When stressful things happen, we want to fight against them; we want to push back. Unfortunately, that's usually impossible, which makes the stress worse. However, our body reacts as if it can push back by developing tension. Maybe that makes us feel just a little bit less powerless.

Maintaining fixed positions. Many people spend a great deal of their time virtually motionless in front of a TV screen or computer. These fixed positions can lock tension into muscles as we get used to holding ourselves in that position and find it hard to relax again afterwards. Often these fixed positions are accompanied by stress (and TV program and film makers are experts at creating emotional tension) and so we subconsciously tighten up even more than we need to. As the tension is subconscious we don't know it's there so we can't release it afterwards.

Sports training causes tension – particularly where the sport requires constant repetitive movements in specific joints, such as cycling or rowing. The wider and freer the range of movements that are used in a sport or activity, the better for the body as a whole. Activities such as dance and martial arts, which have a wide range of movements and stress no particular set of muscles constantly, are highly beneficial. They also enable physical expression – at least dance and the more traditional martial arts do – and physical expression is something that many people lack. Healthy physical expression is excellent at releasing pent-up emotions effectively. Without such an outlet, emotions get tied up in the body and buried in tense muscles.

Day-to-day activities. The way you live your life generates tensions. Always carrying a bag over the same shoulder will build more tension on one side of the body than the other. Your occupation may require you to perform the same movements day in, day out and so on. Again, these will cause imbalances that, over time, will lead to a loss of energy and shortening of your useful life span. Here, again, regularly engaging in a variety of different movements keeps the body fit and agile. As they say in China, 'flowing water does not rot, nor a door hinge rust'.

The true answer to why you have so much tension is, of course, a combination of these things. Tensing your muscles when under stress makes you feel more comfortable, more stable, better protected and prepares your body for action. Unfortunately, you have evolved to face grave dangers followed by periods without danger, so the tension is supposed to be followed by relaxation.

Your stress is often so continuous that you may have learned to maintain the tension from a young age and continued that bad habit for the rest of your life.

The problem here is that we can tense muscles with both the conscious and subconscious parts of our minds. We may wish to relax a muscle consciously, but our subconscious, wishing to keep us protected, maintains some tension in the muscle. When a muscle becomes chronically tight, it forgets what it is like to be lengthened and so it can no longer do its job with the same efficiency. Its range of movement becomes shorter and shorter and it also becomes weaker. This leads to other muscles in the same area having to work extra hard to take some of its workload. These supporting muscles then become tense and overloaded and can also suffer overuse injuries, become painful and add to the strain in that general area. The tension spreads as the body desperately does what it can to maintain a state of balance.

How do you relax?
When asked this question, a whole range of answers come forth. There are a wide range of methods and practices, products and services to help people relax. In fact, it's a huge industry. With so many methods on offer, you'd imagine that nobody could possibly still be stressed. However, you know and I know and the people who sell you those stress relief products and services also know that what they are selling you can only work in the short term, at best. What they don't tell you (probably because they don't know themselves) is exactly *why* that is.

Why on earth is long-lasting, genuine, deep relaxation so difficult to attain? The answer is the 'tension paradox' but, before we look at what that is, let's take a quick look at your relaxation options.

Here are some of the main things people do to relax and release some of their stress. Here I also tell you why they don't really work.

> *Alcohol.* Alcohol is a muscle relaxant and a natural accompaniment to enjoying yourself socially. Unfortunately, like all substances that chemically change your physiology, more and more is required to gain the same effect. Also, when the alcohol wears off your tension levels return to normal. So, no gain there, apart from the party fun you had.

> *Recreational drugs.* These work on changing your brain chemistry to make you feel fantastic. However, clearly this is similar to alcohol, but even more addictive and a lot more expensive. It's still a short-term high.

> *Smoking.* Much the same here again. The other advantage that smoking has is that the smoker learns to inhale deeply. Sure, the air he inhales is full of toxins, but a full and slow exhalation is very powerful in releasing tension. We will cover this more in Chapter 4, but for now be aware that if you're a smoker looking to give up then learning breathing exercises will help you enormously in kicking your habit successfully.

> *Holidays.* A change is as good as a rest, or so they say. Unfortunately, holidays can also be stressful. I see them more as a way of exploring the world than a way to relax. As a relaxation option, they are short-term and expensive.

> *Sports and recreational pastimes.* This is more like it. The best activities are the ones that enable you to move your body freely in a wide range of movements rather than using the same movements continuously. However, all kinds of exercise help move the body, challenge the heart and lungs and make you feel better about yourself. The effects last over the long term, as

long as you keep at it. As for expense? Well, that's up to you. There are many free ways to keep fit and healthy.

Hot baths/saunas etc. The heat relaxes your muscles, making you feel temporarily good and possibly somewhat more pain-free. Naturally, when the body cools down the tensions build up again.

Country walks. Fresh air and exercise. I love country walks, but find that they are more beneficial and fun if I'm walking and breathing efficiently and have some awareness and knowledge of the countryside I'm travelling through.

Pampering. No longer just for the girls. Pampering is a big business, with all kinds of spa breaks on offer. Of course, you could just have a haircut and manicure. It's good for making you feel better about yourself and taking your mind off your woes as long as you realise that, again, it's short term and not exactly cheap.

Don't expect to find peace around you until you can find the peace inside you.

So, if none of these are able to give us any long-term relief of tension, does that mean we're doomed to remain a prisoner of our tensions for the rest of our lives? No, of course not! But before we go on to look at long-term strategies, let's take a look at the all-important reason *why* none of the above can offer anything more than short-term relief.

What is the 'tension paradox'?

Tensing a muscle is easy. It's an active process that can be done consciously or subconsciously. You can consciously choose to tense your biceps or stomach muscles, and can feel the results. You can choose to make the contraction stronger or less strong. You can choose to hold the muscle in maximum contraction.

Unfortunately, relaxing a muscle is not so easy. You relax a muscle by not contracting it any more. Therefore it is a passive process. You have no idea whether the muscle is fully 100% relaxed just 50% or even barely 10%. There is no way of knowing, as you get no feedback.

You can feel that you're not actively tensing it any more but you cannot feel whether it has regained its full former length. It's hard enough trying to relax a muscle that you have tensed consciously, but most of our tension is held subconsciously, and so we have very little idea of which muscles are tensed and how much they are tensed.

This is what I call the 'tension paradox': the inability to feel how relaxed any muscle or part of the body is, added to the inability to increase muscle length, i.e. to be able to relax it consciously.

Relaxing a muscle is a passive process with no feedback.

The tension paradox explains why virtually everyone on this planet lives in a state of excess tension over which they have little or no control. We have seen why we hold on to so much tension. Now let's take a quick look at how that tension spreads around the body.

As we all know, the body is held in position and mobilised by the action of muscles. A healthy muscle is one that can move a joint in a full range of movement and is able to contract, then relax again, efficiently. The muscles work together to hold the skeleton upright and then to move it as necessary.

The human muscular system is extremely complicated. There are around 600–750 distinct muscle units in the human body. The brain has to control each of these muscles every moment of every day. It has to ensure that when you reach out to pick up your toothbrush exactly the right muscles fire in the correct order, with each muscle moving the joint the precise amount and with the exact amount of force. If the brain gets any of these extraordinary calculations wrong then your movements will be unbalanced and jerky.

A simple act like picking up a toothbrush requires muscles in the hands, arms, back, shoulders and chest to move to extend the arm, and the muscles in the lower body to remain toned to prevent you collapsing. They should also be responsive to any changes in balance, such as the extra weight in front of the body from your extended arm, and be able to compensate for this smoothly and quickly. The calculations that your brain makes every second of every day just to keep you upright and moving would put the best supercomputers to shame. Yet all of this is made so much harder when your posture is holding onto unnecessary tensions.

Excess tension in any muscle prevents that muscle from fulfilling its role efficiently. This means that other muscles that do similar jobs will sometimes have to take up some of the workload of that muscle. The other muscles may then become overworked and become more liable to injury, particularly if they are being used to generate force at different angles than they are used to, or designed for. If a muscle is overly tight with tension, then it will pull on the joint.

The unwinnable tug-of-war contest

Every muscle has an opposite number on the other side of the joint to counter its forces. This is called the antagonist. The triceps, which straighten your elbow, are the antagonists for the biceps, which bend your elbow. If your biceps are holding on to tension then the elbow would naturally bend unless there was compensatory tension in your triceps to prevent it (which there is). These opposing muscles are much like a tug-of-war team, both pulling on the joint to either keep it stable or to move it. However, they are both pulling far more than is necessary and thus wasting a lot of their energy in the process.

The tug-of-war competition is occurring in every joint in your body, and this puts a huge strain on your muscles and joints and drains you of energy.

As muscles on one side of a joint tighten they create excess tension on the other side, which strains the muscles and tendons to breaking point. Eventually, when they can take no more, even the smallest, most innocent movement can cause one of those muscles or tendons to tear.

The most amazing part of all this is that this tug of war is going on all over your body all the time and yet you are almost completely oblivious to it. Every movement you make is being opposed by muscles that would normally move the joint the opposite way. Hence an enormous amount of energy is wasted all the time, partly through the tug-of-war game and partly through the need to maintain these tensions 24 hours a day.

Every position you stand or sit in, every movement becomes a compromise between using the muscle fibres that aren't already locked up in the tug-of-war contest to position and move your body as best they can.

It's important to note here that it is a waste of time releasing tension in specific muscles unless you also release tension in the opposite muscles (known as antagonists). Otherwise it would be like trying to release tension on a rope by asking just one tug-of-war team to stop pulling so hard. They would instantly feel the rope being pulled away from them and so would increase their pulling force again to stop the rope moving. The only way to release the tension on the rope is to persuade both sides to pull more gently. This information is of particular importance to those who stretch regularly and to massage therapists. Unless you remove the tension evenly, much of your work will be undone in a very short time.

Remember to always release tension in the muscles on both sides of a joint.

My training in massage therapy taught me that an injury or area of tension in a part of a muscle quickly causes tension in the surrounding ones as well. The whole area can become very tense, making it very difficult for you – or a therapist – to feel where the problem originates. This problem, added to the tug-of-war problem mentioned earlier, means that tension will gradually spread throughout your entire body.

Tension is never local to just one muscle but always spreads in an attempt to either spread the working load or in an attempt to balance the body. However, the tension paradox tells us that we can't feel it happening and couldn't easily prevent it even if we could.

So, before you or your physical therapist can work on any specific area they have to release enough tension in the surrounding muscles to identify where the source of the problem is. You will probably know from experience that if you have a shoulder problem then the whole shoulder feels stiff and painful. Often it's difficult to pinpoint the exact area of the problem.

Even if you could pinpoint an area, that doesn't mean that you have found the origin of the problem, only the area that is shouting the loudest. The only sensible answer here is to release the tensions that are causing the pain in the first place (or contributing to the continuous feelings of pain). But how can we release those tensions when we aren't sure which part of the body the pain originates from?

When any part of your body is locked up with tension, it makes it much harder to feel what is going on in that area. The tension prevents the free flow of neurological information to and from your brain. This is hugely important to know for two reasons. First, your subconscious mind may well have created tension in that area with the sole purpose of preventing you from feeling what is going on there.

Many people are unaware that tension is often due to repressed feelings associated with being hurt in the past. It's not just the feelings that are repressed and buried in the tensions, but the actual memories associated with the event as well. I know from the various kinds of physical therapy that I have done over the years that a release of tension often accompanies a release of emotions and repressed memories. It's as if you have a painful memory in your hand so you lock your fist tightly around it so that you never need look at or deal with it. The problem with this is that you can't let go of it either.

The second reason is that the simple act of using your mind to feel what is going on inside your body will start to release tensions in that part of the body. You can try this for yourself now. Mentally feel your left collarbone. Don't just visualise it but put your mind inside it and feel it. Try to feel the whole length of it. While you are doing this, pay attention to the sensations you can feel around there. My bet is that you will have felt at least some release of tension in the local muscles.

The very act of focusing on a part of your body forces your muscles to release tension to increase the flow of information to your brain.

So you may have subconsciously created tensions to suppress feelings and memories, but by consciously using your mind to feel your body from the inside you can reverse the process, release the tension and free those stuck feelings and memories. This isn't as easy as it sounds, though. It could take

31

weeks, months or even years of trying. But in the process you will release a lot of tension and get to know yourself and your body very well indeed.

Pain and physical tension

Pain is caused either by a disease that changes our internal structure, a tearing of skin or other soft tissue or, most commonly, by intolerable tension.

Pain affects everybody. In this brief section I will explain to you my theories of pain and pain relief. There are two types of pain, acute and chronic. I believe that virtually all chronic pain and a significant percentage of acute pain have the same cause. Let me explain the difference.

Acute pain is caused by a recent trauma. That trauma will have caused external or internal bleeding and the pain will continue until the wound has healed and the structure, e.g. skin or muscle, is no longer leaking your precious red stuff all over the place.

Chronic pain is often misdiagnosed. It is the pain that comes on gradually or suddenly with no obvious cause. We're talking about anything from migraines to arthritis to repetitive strain injury (RSI) to back pain. Chronic pain lasts a long time, hence the word chronic. The pain can, potentially, last for years because its cause is the intolerable, unceasing strain placed on the soft tissues of your body.

Essentially, acute pain comes on suddenly and there is usually an identifiable cause such as an injury. It can be mild or severe and may last moments or go on for months.

Chronic pain persists long after the original injury has healed.

The pain signals in chronic pain remain active in the nervous system and so the tension in the muscles doesn't let go, causing decreased mobility and loss of energy. One of the aims of this book is to enable you to release pain, both chronic and acute, and also to speed up the healing process.

Muscular tension restricts circulation of the blood, which then deprives tissues of the oxygen they so desperately need, particularly if they have been injured. This tension puts extra strain on the heart as it works harder to push sufficient blood through the restricted blood vessels. It also means that the waste products of metabolism, which are normally flushed away with the blood, build up in the muscles which can be another cause of pain.

A long-term restriction of circulation, which is commonly seen in the modern world, causes the elastic component of tissues to become less elastic and to shrink. Thus a normal range of healthy movement is hindered and an attempt to move to or beyond the range of this restricted movement results in more pain. Gradually, as the years go by, the amount of physical movement we are capable of becomes more and more limited, and pain can become a constant companion.

Pain is your body's way of trying to tell you something. Often it's the result of a chronic tightness in a muscle that causes the muscle to go into spasm. This tightness can originate from overuse of the muscle, an injury or may have an emotional cause, where tensions in the mind get stored in the body, as I mentioned earlier.

These tensions have been building up in you since early childhood, and the layers of tension gradually build up on top of each other, preventing efficient movement. If you had a greater awareness of what was going on inside then you could feel this tension building up and could take steps to reverse it, but you can't feel it and don't listen, and so the tension keeps building up and will eventually cause chronic pain. The pain, of course, is your body shouting at you that it can't take any more tension in that area. The usual response to this is to shut up that shouting voice by taking some painkillers. However, they may quieten the voice for a while but it soon starts shouting again, so more painkillers are needed to keep the part of you that is in pain shut up. This is a vicious cycle.

The source of chronic pain is almost never at the site of the pain. but releasing tension anywhere in that area will help to reduce the pain.

This book will teach you how to release tension in specific areas of the body. This will help enormously in controlling pain and speeding up the healing process. Remember that most of these tense problem areas are both unknown to you right now and also surrounded by other areas of high tension. They have probably also been around for years and you have been hanging on to them out of habit. So we will need to learn every skill in this book to track them down and release them successfully. Despite all this, some of these tense areas will resist all attempts to release them and that is usually because they are serving a purpose right now in your life. These you won't be able to release until you have resolved the issues that are maintaining that tension inside you.

In this chapter we have seen that the real cause of your distress is not stress but tension. Tension is not easy to get rid of as the tension paradox tells us we cannot feel it build up and have little idea of where inside us it is developing at any given moment. Tension is our enemy, but in learning how to reduce it we will learn a lot about ourselves. We can learn to regain physical skills as well as mental faculties, we can rediscover our youthful vitality and bid farewell to many niggling health problems. The little work that is required is more than compensated for by these wondrous benefits. Read on to find out more.

Let's finish this chapter with a simple exercise to release tension in the neck and shoulders – a very common place to hold tension. We will be simply using the force of gravity and allowing our arms to relax downwards. This is hard to do from our normal 'arms hanging down' position so instead we will put the weight of our arms above our shoulders.

The arm hang exercise

1. Raise both arms above your head.

2. Keeping them above your head, relax them downwards and allow the weight of your arms to push your shoulder blades downwards. Maintain the position for at least 10 seconds and keep focusing on relaxing downwards. The longer you hold the position the better, as gradually you will feel the tension let go and your shoulders droop.

3. Crucially, at the end of the exercise don't just drop your arms quickly but lower them slowly, elbows first, and focus on keeping your shoulder blades relaxed downwards. If you do it too quickly they will pop back up into their habitual position and you will have lost the benefit of the exercise. Lower your elbows then your hands slowly, keeping your shoulders down.

At the end of this exercise you should feel as if your shoulders are several inches lower than they normally are. If possible, try not to move them for a few minutes afterwards, and let them get used to being in this new, lower position. Feels great, doesn't it?

A summary of Chapter 2

The stresses you face in your life cause your muscles to tense up. You cannot feel this process happening, so cannot control it. That is the tension paradox.

This tension affects every aspect of your life – your health, your wellbeing, your emotions and how you feel about yourself. It will play a major role in your future health and useful life expectancy.

These tensions are the major cause of chronic pain. Only by releasing the tensions that are tearing you apart can a long-term release of pain ever be possible.

CHAPTER 3

The Expansion Principle

In this chapter

> If the tension paradox is stopping me from being able to relax, then how on earth can I release my tensions?
>
> I need specific exercises to help me release my overall tension load and also to target specific areas that trouble me. Can you help?
>
> I have released tension in one area, but now another area feels very tight. What's going on and how do I progress?

All your stress is based on fear and that fear contracts your body and your mind, which prevents you from living your life to the fullest. Your stress leads to tension which contracts your body and mind, making you ever more susceptible to stress which causes more tension, leading to more contraction, and so on.

The tension paradox prevents you from feeling where you are contracted, so it is extremely difficult to escape the vicious circle of stress, tension and contraction. This chapter does nothing less than show you an escape route; a tried and tested method for beating the tension paradox. It's a practical chapter with several exercises to help you open yourself up again and start to free yourself from your tension prison.

Stress is fear

All stress is based on fear. Think about any of the situations in which you feel stressed. In every case, fear is behind the pain. Stressed at work? Meet the fears of not having the mental and physical resources to do your job properly, leading to the fear of being overlooked or demoted or even losing your job. Stressed at home? Meet the fears of not being able to be yourself, not being seen to be a good parent, not being respected and having your opinion valued by your family. All of our stresses have their roots in the debilitating state known as fear and when we feel fear we react as many animals do – we retreat inside ourselves.

When a tortoise is threatened, it retreats into its shell. There it is protected from physical attack and so it can feel safe. Us humans have no shell and so our bodies are relatively vulnerable to attack. Each animal has its own defence mechanisms: some use speed, some power, some take flight, others use camouflage. Humans have no particular advantages in these areas, but we have something that no other animal possesses: a reasoning brain.

Your brain is your greatest asset and in a way it is like your tortoise shell. When you feel under threat you retreat inside your mind in the same way the tortoise retreats into its shell. This is more literally true than you may think. When you are threatened or under pressure, you contract inward and upward towards your head, which leaves much of your body tense. You may not have noticed this, but you instinctively know it to be true. Your shoulders raise, you breathe more shallowly, higher into your chest, your legs contract upwards, leaving them feeling weak and shaky. When panicked, your arms shoot up towards your face and a sudden sharp in-breath pulls in your stomach and sets the tension there. Our language is replete with examples of this behaviour: 'That made me jump', 'I could feel my hackles raise and my hair stand on end', 'He really gets my back up', 'Why are you acting so jumpy?'

One of the aims of this book is to help you dissociate from yourself in times of pressure. When you feel yourself stressed, angry or fearful, then try to take a step back with part of your mind and observe yourself objectively and how you are reacting physically and mentally. If you are caught up in the drama of the situation it becomes hard to control yourself, but if you get used to mentally dissociating a part of yourself and using that to observe your reactions, you can then learn about how you react to help change that reaction into one that is more appropriate and healthy. This is so important.

All of this book is about teaching you skills to deal with stress and release tension and a set of principles that will help you to lead a happier and healthier life. However, if you cannot help but get totally caught up in your dramas then you won't remember these skills until it's too late, by which time you'll be awash with tension and mentally in tatters.

The first and most important of these principles is understanding how to escape the tension paradox.

Escaping the tension paradox

Let's quickly remind ourselves of what the tension paradox is. When a muscle is contracted, it shortens. If we have consciously contracted that muscle, we will feel it shortening but when we release the muscle all we can feel is the emptiness of the contraction that used to be. We have no way of knowing how far the muscle has regained its original length, if at all. This is the paradox of tension – the fact that we can consciously tense a muscle, but relaxing a muscle is a passive process from which we get no feedback.

I was considering this paradox one sleepless night, when an extraordinary idea came to me. If we can tense a muscle by sending an order from the brain to contract it, can't we relax a muscle by sending it an order to expand and lengthen? I tried this while lying in bed that night and was amazed by the results. Clearly, there was still a lot of tension which had solidified over the years, but some of the more pliable tension, or soft tension, responded quite quickly to my mental orders to expand. All I had to do was mentally see and feel the area in question opening up, expanding and lengthening.

Mentally expanding an area releases tension.

This is a discovery that has far-reaching consequences. It now becomes clear that there is a mechanism available to us to lengthen and soften our musculature as well as to contract and harden it. This lengthening mechanism seems to be not as strong as the contracting mechanism, but perhaps that is because it is one that is never practised. Like all physical skills, once the brain has learned it and strengthened the neural pathways then the mechanism will become stronger and more efficient. Finally we can take some measure of power over our levels of tension and, therefore, also of stress.

How and why are we contracted?

Life seems to be a continuous process of contraction. We contract our muscles when we're stressed, contract our minds when frightened or confused. Fear also prevents us from going outside our comfort zone, and we often contract inside ourselves when faced with having to communicate with our fellow man.

This gradual but continuous contraction into ourselves serves the purpose of making us feel safe and secure when we feel under threat, but the drawbacks are huge. By and large, we no longer know who we are as our sense of self is so small and contracted. We have little – if any – knowledge of what's going on inside us; our relationships with other humans and our environment is often based on fear, rather than any kind of genuine connection, and our bodies are so stiff with contracted, tense muscles that we suffer a huge panoply of ills. Not knowing what to do to sort out these ills and not having the ability to look inside ourselves to find the cause, we turn to our medical industry for a pill to swallow to make the pain temporarily go away.

We live in a state of contraction due to fear.

Fear causes our muscles to tense and tighten up, thus preventing us from going further into danger. The contraction of the muscles becomes habitual and thus permanent. The contraction is also mental, locking us into our own world and preventing us from making any real connection with others. This lack of connections extends to a lack of feeling about others and also our environment.

We read in the newspapers stories about various kinds of damage done to the environment, as well as the terrible things people do to each other, but our contracted state prevents us from feeling any real pain and thus from caring too much. However, it is partly this media bombardment of tragedy that is to blame, as nobody who is open to the world around him can cope with the knowledge of all the bad things that are going on everywhere. The media consider it their role to give us all the bad news they can find, repeated and exaggerated as necessary, only marginally balanced with a few fun items occasionally to lighten the mood. Most news items don't affect us personally and so we are probably better off not knowing about them, as they increase the gradual build-up of stress and tension in our lives. Naturally, this excess tension makes us more susceptible to stress and so the cycle goes on.

We are contracted physically, emotionally, mentally and spiritually, and kept in a prison that is largely of our own making. Inside the prison, it is cold and dark and we survive on a few scraps. Learn how to expand the walls of your prison until they dissolve altogether, releasing you into the bright and warm sunlight and a world overflowing with abundance and goodness. Read on to find out how.

As I mentioned earlier, contracting a muscle can be an active process; i.e. you can make your bicep contract via a nerve signal from the brain. More often, though, contraction is a passive process as it happens to you without you even realising it. We also know by now that we cannot force a muscle to relax: that can only be a passive process. But can we make it a more efficient passive process?

Yes, we can, and the answer is to use the power of your mind to create an imaginary force with which we align ourselves. The process is simple and can be done from any sitting or standing position, although it works best from the stress-proof posture which we'll examine in Chapter 6. The exercise I will share with you now uses this passive process to strengthen your posture and, at the same time, help to release tension in any areas where it isn't needed. This exercise is for the whole body but it can easily be modified if you wish to focus on any particular part.

One of the most popular relaxation exercises is called progressive muscle relaxation. Many of you may be aware of this exercise. In brief, you lie on the floor and focus on each body part in turn, tensing them hard for a few seconds and then releasing them. This initial hard tensing causes the muscle to release a bit more of its usual tension in order to recover. This exercise is prescribed and used all around the world. It is a good exercise and one that I have used myself. However, with the knowledge that you now have, you can see its limitations. Even after a muscle has been fully tensed, there is still no way of knowing how much it has regained its length after the tension is released. All you are doing is using its recovery from tension to trick it into lengthening more than usual.

A more efficient and powerful way to achieve the same thing, as we have seen, is to send a message from the brain for the muscle to lengthen. This message can be done as either a verbal message to lengthen, open, expand and so on or by mentally feeling the body in that area and imagining it expanding or by visualising the area expanding and opening – or preferably all three. Some people have difficulty in feeling parts of themselves, while others have difficulty in visualising what's going on inside them.

Progressive muscle expansion exercise

This exercise is identical to progressive muscle relaxation except that, instead of tensing the muscle concerned and then releasing the tension, you focus on expanding and lengthening the area concerned.

1. Lie on your back on the floor with your legs uncrossed and your hands by your sides so that no part is touching any other and you can relax fully.

2. Start with your feet. They have to cope with the forces of carrying you around all day and, particularly if your posture is poor and unbalanced, may not be able to support the body as they should. As a result they're often abused and neglected.

3. Focus your attention on your feet and imagine them expanding, growing, lengthening. As your mind sends these images and commands to your feet, the muscles will start to release tension, since that is the only way the feet can grow. Eventually you will feel them become warm or tingly as the muscles relax and the blood flow improves.

4. Move your attention to your lower legs and again imagine them expanding and lengthening. The calf muscles also take a lot of your weight continuously and our sitting position means they are often tighter than they should be.

5. Focus on your knees. Knee problems are common. The knee is supported by many muscles, tendons and ligaments but excess tension in those areas can put intolerable strains on the joint, particularly if those forces misalign the joint to the side. Pay

attention to inside the knee joint, and imagine it expanding outwards.

6. Move your attention up to your upper legs and hips, where most of the strongest muscles in your body are located. As these muscles are larger and many are deep down and close to the bone, you should spend longer on this area, feeling them expand in all directions. It may take some time before you feel the relaxing benefits but they will definitely come.

7. Next focus on your waist, between your hips and your ribs. Here many of your deepest and earliest tensions are located. These tensions can play havoc with your digestion and energy levels. Breathe deep down into your lower abdomen and feel the whole area expand and relax. Allow the expansion to go in all directions: forward towards the ceiling, backwards into the ground, out to the sides plus up and down. Expand and relax.

8. Next we have the ribs and upper back. The rib cage holds the heart and lungs and is usually surrounded by very tight muscles. The chest muscles wage a constant war with the back muscles, which stresses the heart and lungs. Open it up, relax and expand. You should feel your shoulder blades relaxing more easily onto the ground as your tensions dissolve.

9. Shoulders next. We all know how tense they can get. Include the neck with this exercise. Feel the whole line from the ears to the shoulders lengthening, and from the chin to the sternum. Similarly, feel the back of the head to the mid-back relax and lengthen. That should feel really good.

10.Now the arms and hands. You know the drill by now. Lengthen, expand, relax all the way down to the hands and fingers. Your hands are also likely to start tingling or feeling warm. Welcome this sensation, as it means you are relaxing and your circulation is improving.

11. Now spend a few minutes trying to expand your whole body at the same time, all the way from the top of the head to the tips of the feet and the fingers. Let everything expand away from everything else.

Although this exercise is best done lying down, it can be done in any position at any time. Try it while you're sitting at your desk, or in any other situation where you are able to focus your mind on your body for a few minutes. You will soon learn to increase your relaxation under any circumstances.

Warning 1

Don't try to expand the skull on its own. That can make some people feel very sick very quickly. It's fine when done as a general expansion as the focus is everywhere and so it is less powerful.

Warning 2

The effects of this exercise, like all the exercises in this book, is temporary. The effects will last, at the most, an hour or so and, at the least, a few seconds. 'What's the point, then?' I hear you ask. Well, regular practice makes the effects last longer. Gradually the body learns another way to be. It discovers that it can shed the tensions it's hanging on to for dear life.

Remember, when you become familiar with this exercise you can do it any time, anywhere. You can focus on specific troublesome areas or just do the final point and mentally expand your entire body in one go. This will help you to quickly gain a level of relaxation that most people find impossible. Using this one skill will help you to cope with the 'slings and arrows of outrageous fortune' with equanimity. Practise it again and again, and it will change your life.

Five-point expansion exercise

This version is a quick way to release general tension. You simply focus on your extremities and visualise them expanding. This can be done standing, sitting or lying down.

1. Bring your attention to the five periphery points – the top of your head, both hands and both feet.

2. Imagine that each of these points is being gently pulled away from your centre. Your head is being pulled into the air, your feet down onto the ground and your hands are being pulled in alignment with your arms.

There can be no doubt that regular practice of these expansion exercises will see a reduction in your general tension levels. Remember that just doing it once or twice will only have very short-term effects. Your aim must be to re-educate your body into being able to function without the need to hold on to its excess tension.

I feel tension or pain. What should I do?

Sometimes this exercise may make some people feel more tense and painful than before. Why is this? Well this exercise makes you focus your attention on what is going on inside you. Now that you are paying attention you will notice other areas of pain and tension that you hadn't noticed before. Now you can hear them shouting at you. They were shouting with pain before, but you just weren't listening.

As you know by now, virtually all pain is as a result of tension. If you can release enough of your tension, then your body will be more balanced and the areas which were feeling intolerable strains can stop shouting their pain signals at you. Try the local expansion exercise. to release tension in specific areas of your body.

Local expansion exercise

The process is as follows.

1. Scan your body for areas of tension.

2. Keep your attention on the area and expand it until something changes.

3. Stay with whatever changes and keep expanding.

Let's take these steps one at a time.

Scan the body for areas of tension

Focus on the area of pain or tension and mentally feel the surrounding area, starting at the surface then going as deep as you are able. To start with, you will find this difficult but with practice you will be able to scan deeper and more accurately. You will be able to go deeper and deeper inside, eventually feeling the organs, the blood vessels, bones etc. You are trying to find any areas that feel painful, tight, numb, hot or cold – in fact, any sensation that feels like there may be a problem. It's usually advisable to build up your experience on smaller problem areas first rather than the most painful place you have at the moment. You may be amazed that releasing seemingly small areas can have dramatic effects on other parts of you anyway. The reason for this is that all parts are connected internally, so a release of tension in any part will release tension to a greater or lesser degree in all other parts.

Keep your attention on the area and expand it until something changes

Here I want you to not only keep your attention on the area, but to mentally place your attention inside the area and try to expand outwards. Imagine you have created a small cavity at the centre of the area and you are now gently expanding that cavity outward in all directions. It is more powerful to use your breathing and focus together. As you breathe in, expand the area and maintain the same feeling of expansion as you breathe out (this is known as the expansion breath, and we'll cover it in the next chapter). Keep breathing and expanding until you feel the change.

Stay with whatever changes and keep expanding

As you continue to breathe and keep your focus on that one area, you are likely to feel it change. This change could be in a number of ways.

You may feel the area become warmer

Your breathing and mental focus has brought lots of energy and oxygen to that area. The warmth will help to dissolve the tension in the same way a hot bath or massage does. As the tension in the surrounding muscles dissolves you should be able to pinpoint the area of the problem more precisely.

You may feel the pain or tension start to lessen

This is good. It means you are probably working at or near the site of the problem and it's responding well. If it responds quickly it may be fairly recent tension you're holding on to. Be aware that you may still tense up the area out of habit, so may need to work on that area a few more times before you're completely free of it.

You may feel the pain or tension increase

It isn't really increasing; it only seems to increase because you're now paying attention to it. It's as if someone is shouting in a room and you open the door to find out what's going on. Opening the door makes the shout seem louder; it doesn't mean the pain has got worse or the shout has actually got louder. Maintain your attention there and keep expanding. The pain will eventually diminish and go away. If it doesn't, it either isn't due to muscular tension at all or it is tension but you're focusing on the wrong place, or the tension is caused by some emotional problem that is in your life right now that you need to deal with.

You may feel the pain or tension move to another area

What is happening here is that some tension is being released from the area and another area nearby is taking up the job of stabilising the body that the old tense area used to do. This could now be feeling more tense than the area you have just released, so the pain seems to travel to another area. There will still be some residual pain or tension in the first area, so it's a good idea to continue releasing that tension as fully as you can before moving on to the new painful area. Otherwise you will only be releasing the surface tension in each area and it will regain its level of tension (and pain) quite quickly.

What you are aiming to achieve here is a change in how that tense area feels. Generally it will feel hard, like a solid mass, so use your mind to mentally encompass the whole area. Get an idea of its size and shape and then go inside it and expand from within. As the surrounding areas release, you may feel the area of tension become smaller. Gradually you should feel it soften, perhaps only at the edges at first. Eventually it may feel like a warm liquid sensation rather like a rock becoming molten lava. Although it is no longer a solid mass of tension but is now warm and soft, which is rather a nice sensation, keep focusing on it and expanding it until it goes completely. Unless you release it completely, the tension will return.

Some areas can be quite hard to focus on. What can help greatly here is to touch the area lightly with one or two fingers. This helps to keep your attention on the area you are focusing on. Your touch alone can help to open up the tension inside the area. Never underestimate the power of touch.

We seem to be programmed to respond to a loving touch by releasing tension.

Whether it's a professional massage or a mother touching her child to calm her down, the power of touch can be extraordinary. Research has shown that children who grow up in families where physical contact (of the loving sort) is rare seem more likely to have physical and/or emotional problems in later life.

I have used this technique to release painful tension in many areas of my body and taught it to many others, all of whom have benefited greatly from this simple exercise.

What to do if you're bleeding

This exercise can be very powerful, opening up and expanding the tissues and increasing the local blood flow to the area. Because of this, it works well for all types of chronic pain (by which I mean pain that has been ongoing for some time and is not the result of an injury that has occurred in the last couple of days).

It is very important that you don't try to expand any area that is still bleeding, as this will increase the blood flow, which is the exact opposite of what is needed for healing to take place.

If there is an open wound or there is bleeding inside the skin then move on to the contraction exercise below. Bleeding under the skin causes swelling and compresses the tissues, so the area may feel hot and tight even if no swelling occurs. If in doubt, don't try any expansion exercise on the area for at least 24 hours after the swelling has gone down.

There is a simple exercise you can do to speed the healing process when you are bleeding. It is the opposite of the expansion exercise.

The following exercise should not be seen as a replacement for traditional acute wound healing protocols, particularly PRICE, which is an acronym for:

Protection – protect the area from further harm.

Rest – move the area as little as possible, as any movement will increase blood flow.

Ice – apply ice to cool the area and restrict blood flow.

Compression – compress the area to help prevent or impede swelling which can slow down the healing.

Elevation – raise the part of the body as high as possible so that gravity can help restrict the blood flow. You can do the contraction exercise with the area raised, compressed and with ice applied to maximise the effect.

Local contraction exercise

1. Focus on the area where bleeding or swelling is taking place.

2. Imagine the area contracting like a fist being clenched.

3. Visualise the area as becoming white, i.e. devoid of blood.

4. Try to maintain focus for as long as you can; three minutes or more is best.

When you visualise the area contracting, mental signals will be sent to temporarily minimise blood flow to the affected area. You still need some blood there as it carries the building blocks for healing, but generally we prefer our blood to stay inside our blood vessels. Regular practice of the local expansion exercise is a form of this exercise. They both require the maintenance of mental focus on the specific area that needs expanding or contracting. If you can relax a part of your body at will, then you can also contract it if bleeding occurs. Your sense of self-mastery will grow every day.

A powerful way to increase your ability to expand from within is to imagine yourself being pulled in different directions. There is no measurement to the power of the human mind, and it is simple for you to imagine your body or different parts of it being pulled apart. Just imagine a force pulling apart various joints or muscles and then allow yourself to be pulled in that direction; surrender to the force of the pull.

Try applying this principle to the five-point expansion exercise. Just stand up and spend a few moments imagining that your hands, feet and head are being pulled slowly apart. This is powerful and we will return to this principle in other chapters. You can also apply this to local areas of tension and imagine them being pulled like a piece of putty in different directions. Experiment to see what works best for you.

Regular practice of these expansion exercises will create in you the feeling that the Chinese call 'sung'. Sung is a state of muscular tension that is neither limp and lifeless, nor is it tight and over-contracted. It is exactly the right amount of tension to maintain a position without any excess force or tension being used. This is the feeling that you are aiming to cultivate. Imagine if you had a rubber band and you cut it so that it was now one straight piece of rubber. If you hold it by one end, the rest of it would not be straight but would be wavy, partly curled up by its own internal tensions. If you pull it tight, you are creating more tension in the band than is necessary. However, if you pull it just enough so that it becomes straight, then stop before it starts to stretch, then it is now 'sung'.

Sung means that your muscles are now operating as efficiently as they can be. You will quickly be amazed at the difference this makes to how you do mundane things such as picking up shopping bags or vacuuming. By being aware of your tension states and imagining yourself being pulled in different directions and allowing that force to move you, you are now putting far less effort into your everyday tasks than you used to. If you are able to maintain at least part of your attention on those five points then the force of every movement will be balanced throughout your system. Spreading the load in this way saves a lot of wear and tear on the muscles you most commonly use to accomplish each task. And, of course, those are most likely to be the muscles where you are carrying the most tension. So allow your body to be pulled in different directions and use those pulls to power your movements. It will take a little getting used to, but you will quickly start to enjoy the sense of balance, power and grace that you have suddenly gained.

A summary of Chapter 3

Tension causes the body to contract inwards. The obvious answer is to send signals to the body to expand. This lengthens the muscles and combats the encroachment of contraction.

The progressive muscle expansion exercise is a great way to gain full-body relaxation. It will also help you achieve a restful night's sleep.

The local muscle expansion exercise enables you to focus on the problem areas. They will take a lot of work to clear completely, but you should start feeling the benefits very quickly indeed.

Imagine yourself being pulled in different directions during your daily life to help prevent the otherwise inevitable build-up of localised tension/contraction.

CHAPTER 4

The Stressless Breath

In this chapter

> Why do I feel so tired most of the time?

> I get out of breath really quickly. Am I just unfit or is my breathing partly to blame?

> Can my breathing help stop me from getting so panicky?

> If good breathing is so beneficial then why hasn't my doctor told me about it?

> I've got hiccups. Is there a breathing exercise that can help?

In 1931 a Dr Warburg won the Nobel prize for discovering the cause of cancer.

> *'The cause of cancer is no longer a mystery; we know it occurs whenever any cell is denied 60% of its oxygen requirements.' (Prime Cause and Prevention of Cancer by Dr Warburg)*

It's amazing how few people seem to be aware of the extraordinarily important work of this man. It is also astonishing how, given the proven link between oxygen deprivation and cancer, how little research has been done or published about breathing exercises and cancer.

Janet had already had a stressful day and was feeling tired when it happened. She had a big meeting tomorrow on her latest project and was taking the relevant papers and reports home to study so that she would be prepared for all the possible questions and objections they might throw at her. Suddenly a man barged past her from behind, knocking her bag out of her hand and into a puddle. For a second her mind went blank as she stared at her wet bag. Then it struck her that her project was in there, eighteen months of work being ruined even as she watched. She couldn't breathe; she could feel her heart pounding furiously and she felt as if she was suffocating. As she struggled desperately to get air into her lungs she felt the familiar sensation of 'black butterflies fluttering in my brain', as she called it. It was the sign that she was about to lose consciousness, which she then did.

Janet's panic attack wasn't her first and, although stress seemed the likely cause, it was actually her poor posture and particularly her bad breathing habits that caused her, and many thousands of others, to react in such an extreme and inappropriate way to her situation.

Peter was feeling tired, so tired. He had lost his job three months ago and initially had spent a huge amount of time and resources in looking for other positions, filling in forms, ringing old contacts and generally doing whatever he could to get himself back into productive society again. For the last couple of weeks his energy and resources seem to have run down. He was lethargic and seriously lacking in motivation. He got up late, lounged around his flat and couldn't be bothered to do anything. What's the point of finding any more jobs? he thought to himself. I will just be turned down yet again. It's a total waste of time and effort.

Without realising it, Peter's breathing had changed recently. His recently enforced inactivity, both physical and mental, had caused him to reduce his breathing significantly to the point where he was hardly breathing at all. His subconscious mind recognised that his energy needs were low at the moment, so adjusted his breathing accordingly. Unfortunately, it went a little too far in reducing his breathing and Peter, like most people, was unaware that his shallow breathing was actually causing his low energy and motivation.

Your subconscious mind is controlling your breath right now as you read this.

As you know, your breathing controls the oxygen and CO_2 levels in your blood, but it does much more than that. Your subconscious mind is using your breath to maintain certain levels of tension in various parts of your body. It is using your breath to limit the amount of energy you have and to allow certain emotions to run their course. It does a great job of maintaining the person that you are right now. However, I'm assuming you want to be more than you are now. If that is the case, you need to take conscious control of your breathing.

This chapter will explain how and why your breathing is the single most important aspect of your health over which you can take control. It will describe the pure joy of full breathing: the increased sense of self and inner resources, the control over energy levels, stress levels, increased speed of healing. It will tell you how to breathe, where your breath should go, and which parts of your body should be used. It will even give you the world's only workable cure for hiccups!

Perhaps the single most important thing you can do to
improve your health is to learn to breathe more efficiently.

I know from long experience that, however I am feeling right now, I can change it simply by changing my breathing. It is so simple and so fundamental, yet it is largely ignored by Western medicine. The reason for this, I guess, is obvious. It cannot be marketed, it cannot be easily studied (as everyone breathes so control groups would be hard to control) and there is nothing saleable at the end of it.

This is a shame. We are possibly the only culture in world history that hasn't investigated and used breathing as a healing modality. There are major schools of thought in China and India that specialise in breathing – qigong and pranayama, respectively. Shamans, Native Americans and Aborigines all use breathing for health and to control body and mind. The sheer range of breathing practices and philosophies is enormous, as are the benefits, and even powers, that regular practice confers on the practitioner. Here we focus on the benefits to your health, wellbeing and ability to cope with stress. The type of breathing I teach in this chapter is often called natural breathing. It is natural in that it is the way you used to breathe when you left your mother's womb. Since then, your breathing patterns have changed radically and not for the better. If you wish for the energy, speed of healing and lack of tension of a child, then you need to learn to breathe like one.

Some of the problems that can be alleviated with natural breathing include chronic pain, fatigue, poor circulation, lack of sleep, tightness and chest pain, anxiety, sub-clinical depression, postural problems and many more.

The field of breathing should really be researched much more thoroughly. Changing the way you breathe has massive effects on your health and the way you feel about yourself.

The conscious breath

Your breathing is one of the very few autonomous functions of the body over which you can take conscious control. I cannot consciously control my heart muscles to slow down my heart rate or gain control of the smooth muscles around my large colon to digest my food at a different rate. However, I can control the respiratory muscles to change the speed and power of my breathing.

Your subconscious mind is generally in control of your breathing, and it is expert at changing the rate and rhythm of your breath to maintain the person that you are right now. Whether you are angry, depressed or excited, the subconscious mind changes your breathing to maintain and support your physical and emotional needs. It even uses your breathing to maintain specific levels of tension in certain parts of your body which are acting as a defence mechanism.

However, if you want to have more energy, less tension, better control of your emotions, and to be more relaxed, then you cannot allow your subconscious mind to have sole control over your breathing. Your breath is so fundamentally tied in to your emotions and your energy levels that if you want to be more than you are now then you need to take conscious control, for a while at least, of your breathing.

If you aren't controlling your breathing then you are being controlled by your breathing.

This isn't easy to do because we aren't very practised at it. Generally, you will find that it's OK for a few breath cycles but then you'll find you have either over-breathed and released large amounts of CO_2, or under-breathed, so your CO_2 level is low and you are gasping for breath (your automatic breathing rhythm is mostly about maintaining CO_2 levels). Don't worry; it just takes some practice but a key thing to remember when using breath control is not to try to completely breathe in or out, as this will cause more tension than it releases and can do a lot more harm than good. Don't breathe to more than around 70% of your capacity. It may not sound like much but, in reality, most people are only operating on about 30% or less anyway. At this point many people may be shaking their heads and saying that over-breathing leads to anxiety and tension, yet here I am telling people to breathe more. The important point to note here is that it is not the quantity of air that is taken in and released with each breath but *how* the air is taken in that matters.

It will, as I said, take a little while before you are able to consciously change the rhythm of your breathing successfully for a long period of time but, when you understand the benefits, I think you'll find it will be well worth the effort.

Your breathing will have changed dramatically over the course of your life and your once efficient full breath has been reduced to small gasps of air that stand little chance of providing your body with the oxygen it needs to thrive or, more importantly, maintain the correct CO_2 levels to maintain correct blood pH levels. Yes, you are surviving, but not much more than that.

The joys of a full breath

Learning to take a full and natural breath has huge advantages and is probably the most important single thing you can do to improve your general health and the way you feel about yourself. Here are some of the major benefits:

A full breath supplies every cell in your body with the oxygen it needs to survive. Without that oxygen, cells struggle to perform their roles properly and will probably die prematurely. This early cell death uses huge amounts of your resources in having to make new cells. Hence good breathing benefits every single part of your body and all its processes.

Slower breathing promotes deep relaxation, triggering your relaxation response. The act of slowing down your breathing also seems to slow down your brainwaves, leading to a more relaxed and focused state of mind. It also prevents the hyperventilation that can lead to a panic attack. Hyperventilation – breathing quickly and shallowly – means you are breathing out carbon dioxide faster than your body is producing it, which affects the chemistry of your blood. This can have both long-term and short-term effects, such as dizziness, weakness, shortage of breath, muscle spasms and a tingling feeling around the fingers or mouth.

As breathing can be under either automatic or manual control it acts as a bridge between your conscious and subconscious mind. It enables you to target specific areas of your body not normally under conscious control for controlled relaxation.

A full breath starts to increase your 'inner strength'. It strengthens your inner core, making you less susceptible to being influenced by the people or events around you unless you choose to be. You can then start to live your life the way you want to without feeling you have to conform to other people's expectations of you.

Good breathing brings a surplus of energy to your body. With extra energy, you can do more, you can go out and truly live your life. It makes you feel positive and even happy. Without energy, you sit around, barely breathing, and can easily become negative and depressed.

Just as important as any of the above is the fact that, just as your subconscious mind can support and control your emotional states with your breathing rhythms, you can learn to do the same consciously. You can learn to break out of a negative emotional state, gain more control of your energy levels and enter a state of deep calm at will, with just a little practice. If you want to take control of your life, start by taking control of your breathing.

Most people's breathing habits are so poor that it is likely they are depriving themselves of the most important nutrient their body needs every single day.

Are you one of the deprived majority? If you suffer from any of the following, you probably are:

a general feeling of tiredness or lack of energy a lot of the time

sleeping problems

cold hands or feet (poor circulation)

frequent illnesses and slow recovery

confused thought processes and over-thinking/worrying.

If any of these apply to you, then don't worry – you're among the majority of people, and luckily the answer is relatively simple. Best of all, it won't cost you a penny. You already have all the equipment you need; you just need to learn to use it a bit better.

Your body is comprised of cells, trillions of them. Each one of them is a living organism capable of reproducing, taking in energy and excreting waste products. Every cell in your body needs a regular supply of oxygen, which it converts to energy in order to perform its function – whether it is a brain cell, liver cell, blood cell or whatever.

When your breathing is poor and you have a limited supply of oxygen, your mental and physical health suffers and symptoms like the ones above can become apparent. Your feelings of general fatigue may come from the cells needing to work, but without having the resources to do so. Cold hands and feet are a sign that your body is semi-shutting down unimportant areas to ensure that sufficient oxygen flows to the important organs, particularly the liver, brain and heart. Frequent illnesses and/or slow recovery are a result of your immune system being too weak to do its job properly, and both sleeping problems and confusion often stem from a lack of oxygen in the brain to cope with the mental overload of twenty-first century life.

Oxygen and cancer

Every part of your body – organs, hair, skin, brain and so on – is made up of cells. Each requires a constant supply of oxygen to function. To save each cell from having to develop its own breathing apparatus, each cell takes oxygen directly from specialised cells in your blood. It could even be argued that you, as a body, have evolved merely as an efficient way of providing oxygen and nutrients to your cells.

It is efficient but in most humans it could be much more efficient. As mentioned above, most people's breathing habits are poor, with the result that the cells are not being provided with the oxygen they need. A cell that is no longer being provided with oxygen by the body can no longer function effectively or communicate with the body. It starts to burn sugar instead of oxygen. The cell then starts to act by itself and do what it can to survive by multiplying. This is cancer. I will freely admit that there is scant research to link good breathing habits with lowered cancer rates, but it is well known that cancer thrives in an anaerobic environment. Unfortunately, research is expensive, and if there is no chance of a saleable product at the end of it, then finding sponsors for such research may prove difficult.

Your aid to digestion

'Over a third of the British population regularly suffers from digestive problems.'

As everyone knows, your brain is the command and control centre of your body. It sends messages which are conveyed by nerves to control movement, and also coordinates the secretion of hormones that regulate other functions within your organism.

While the brain is the command centre, it is also useful to think of the abdominal area as the engine of the body. It is fuelled by the food and drink we take in. This food is burned in the furnace of our stomach, intestines and so on, and the fire for that furnace should be provided by diaphragmatic breathing which fans the flames and provides the right conditions for effective digestion and assimilation of nutrients. This is, of course, an analogy but a useful one. Deep breathing, using the diaphragm, has the effect of massaging the digestive organs, thus helping the food to pass through (peristalsis). This inner movement also increases blood flow to the area, further improving digestion. So many people today suffer from gastric upsets, IBS and related problems, constipation and so on that could easily be controlled partially or completely with improved breathing practices. The fact is that few people breathe deeply, and so their digestive organs become stagnant, with toxins building up in the colon and elsewhere which eventually seep out into the bloodstream to cause problems throughout the body, from acne to arthritis.

Deep diaphragmatic breathing helps push the digested food through the intestines, massages the liver, spleen and pancreas, and brings fresh blood to the area. All of these effects improve your ability to fully digest food and extract nutrients from it. If you have a healthy digestive system, the food you eat now will take around 18 hours to fully digest. Undigested food can sit in your colon for days, even weeks, and will gradually fester. Many people find that changing their breathing habits gets things moving in the digestive tract and allows them to eliminate much of the foulness that has been building up. This can take months if a lifetime's worth of accumulated poisons have built up.

Before you set out on any journey, it's a good idea to take stock of where you are right now. I want you to spend a few moments focusing on your breath. Don't try to change anything, but just feel where in your body you feel the breath going. Is the breathing smooth? Is the in breath the same as the out breath? Do you breathe in using your mouth or nose, or a combination of the two? Make a note of your findings, then read on.

The nose for breathing, the mouth for speaking

Although it is possible for us to use either nose or mouth for breathing, there are many reasons why the nose is considered the best organ for effective breathing.

Your nose is designed to filter the air of dust, pollen, viruses, bacteria and other impurities. It also warms the air and moistens it before it reaches the lungs. This filtered, warmed and moist air is now in the optimum state for the transfer of oxygen and CO_2. When you breathe in through the mouth, none of this takes place and the air arrives at your lungs unfiltered, cold and dry.

> Nose breathing slows down the breathing rate and so more oxygen can be extracted with each breath. The mouth should only be used when the nose is blocked or where, because of the intensity of exercise, the nose isn't able to supply enough oxygen (see the exercise below).

During mouth breathing, the brain thinks the body is losing CO_2 too quickly and is stimulated to produce mucus and constrict the blood vessels. This leads to poor circulation to the extremities. In fact, all of the body suffers when blood vessels are constricted.

Nose breathing maintains our sense of smell. This is essential for us to taste food effectively and is also tied in to our memory and our behaviour as it is directly related to the hypothalamus. How boring eating would be if we lost our sense of smell!

Hospital studies have established that nocturnal mouth breathing is a primary cause of snoring.

Nose breathing helps prevent over-breathing and hyperventilation (a major cause of anxiety and panic attacks) by slowing down the amount of air entering the lungs.

Nose breathing also prevents your mouth from hanging open, which has never been a cool look!

So always remember use your nose for breathing and your mouth for eating and speaking.

Nose breathing to increase stamina

I teach several kung fu classes per week. At the beginning of each is a warm-up and series of conditioning exercises which I lead. The students then follow me and listen to my instructions. Therefore it's essential that I am not only able to perform these exercises – which can be hard and fast – but that I also have enough breath to be able to give verbal instructions without gasping for air. I discovered long ago that nose breathing can greatly increase my stamina and at the same time reduce how hard an exercise actually feels. It enables me to lead and teach exercise sessions effectively even when a class of students, many of whom are half my age and quite fit, are gasping for breath.

Nasal stamina exercise

To increase your own stamina and reduce your perceived exertion (how hard the exercise feels), follow the simple steps below:

1. Reduce your exercise intensity to a level where you can comfortably breathe through your nose. This may seem far slower than you are used to but, trust me, soon you will be up to the same intensity level and pushing well past it with far greater ease.

2. If you feel yourself going faster or harder and need to open your mouth to breathe, then you are going too hard and must slow down to ensure nose breathing is maintained. You may be astonished at how quickly you can increase the intensity without needing to open your mouth to bring in extra air.

Remember the old Chinese saying – a closed mouth catches no flies!

Earlier I asked you to make a note of the way you habitually breathe. One of the key things from that exploration is where in your body does your breath go?

Most people find that they tend to breathe into the middle or upper part of their chest. Chest breathing is an inefficient means of bringing in oxygen. Some people breathe very high up in their chest, so high that their collar bone (clavicle) moves up and down with the breath. They are called clavicular breathers, and these people tend to be prone to high levels of anxiety and panic attacks.

Your lungs are cone-shaped, with the narrowest part at the top and the widest part at the bottom. Using chest or clavicular breathing can only fill up the top part of the lungs, and so only a small amount of oxygen can be absorbed by the blood. It also means an equally small amount of CO_2 can be breathed out. This means you have to breathe faster to maintain your oxygen and pH levels. You are using the intercostal muscles in your ribs to breathe, and overusing them will cause tension all around the upper body.

To breathe efficiently and so bring in more oxygen to your starving cells, you need to learn to draw air down to the lowest part of your lungs. Fortunately, we have a muscle that is designed to do that job and it happens to be one of the strongest muscles in your body. Unfortunately, in many cases it is used so rarely that it's virtually paralysed from lack of use. It is called the diaphragm.

The muscles of breathing

Let's take a brief look at the muscles involved in the breathing process and how to breathe more efficiently. Note that these are the physiological basics, and there is much more to the breathing process than this.

Your diaphragm is your most important breathing muscle and perhaps the most important muscle in your body. It is a sheet of muscle that stretches across the bottom of the rib cage. When contracted it pulls downward, drawing air deep into the lungs and fully oxygenating the blood. Your diaphragm is such a strong muscle that, when you learn to use it properly, it helps push blood around the lower part of your body, thus acting as a second heart. It has more surface area than the heart muscle and, as it pulls down, it strongly compresses the organs in the abdomen and pushes large amounts of blood through the system. This takes a large load off your heart and, with practice, can help reduce your heart rate and normalise blood pressure.

Basically, when you inhale you should use your diaphragm to pull air into the bottom of the lungs and expand your chest to complete the inhalation. The chest muscles (intercostals) are really secondary to the diaphragm so, at rest, it is often just the diaphragm that is necessary for the breathing process. To exhale you reverse the process, relaxing the chest muscles and the diaphragm. This will shrink the chest cavity, pushing air out of your lungs. There is a problem here, though, and it is to do with our old friend, the tension paradox. To exhale is again a passive process; you breathe out by releasing tension in the diaphragm and intercostals, but how do you know how relaxed they have become? Of course you can't, as you know from the tension paradox.

Your diaphragm is probably holding on to more tension than any other muscle in your body.

Most people barely use their diaphragm at all as it is so rigid with tension. This is a shame, as your diaphragm is one of the most powerful muscles in your body.

The reason why your diaphragm is probably frozen with tension is simple – it is stress. When you are under stress, one of your natural instincts is to hold your breath. I'm sure you have noticed this. You can go several seconds without breathing and without even noticing that you're holding your breath. Hence the diaphragm contracts and stays contracted at the slightest sign of stress. Gradually it loses its flexibility and thus its function. More and more, your breathing takes place higher up in the chest, with the diaphragm occasionally waking up to assist in a big yawn.

For some people, deep diaphragmatic breathing can be a bit scary as it feels as if you are exposing a vulnerable part of yourself, but you must work through this if you are to progress. As I mentioned in the introduction, the body and mind are reflections of each other and opening up the deepest parts of the body can open up the deepest recesses of the mind. It is possible that you may regain memories of past traumatic episodes, experience nightmares or sudden emotional releases such as bouts of anger or tearfulness. Often these traumatic events occurred at a time when you weren't emotionally mature enough to deal with the trauma, and so you locked it away deep inside you until you were better able to deal with the pain.

If you have a good support system such as family and close friends who can help you through this, then now may be that day. It is unlikely, however, that much emotional trauma will be stirred up by the breathing process but it is wise to take note of your emotional stability when you first start opening up and breathing into the abdomen. Believe me, I'm not trying to put you off attempting this. The advantages of good breathing far outweigh the unlikely outcome of having to deal with some repressed emotions.

Another reason why the diaphragm gets little use is our obsession with having a flat belly. Abdominal breathing means there is a slight expansion of the stomach area in all directions as we inhale, then it returns to the usual position. It isn't really noticeable, but for many people the idea of letting their stomach out is a big no-no. This isn't really a good excuse for not belly breathing for, as we shall see, correct breathing and posture will actually make you look and feel slimmer and tone your stomach muscles as well.

The relaxation of the intercostals and the diaphragm is not the end of the exhalation process. We should also get into the habit of using our abdominal muscles to push a little more air out with every breath. This also has several benefits. It empties the lungs further which allows more oxygenated air to be processed, it further massages the internal organs, thus keeping them functioning more efficiently, and it maintains tone in our abdomen – which, in itself, is a fitness goal for many people.

For these reasons, the diaphragm tends to be used very little by the majority of people. Generally those who do use it have to be re-taught to do so in qigong or yoga classes. Let's change that right now and see if we can get that large and powerful muscle moving.

In all the following breathing exercises, remember the 70% rule. Don't attempt to force as much air in or out as you can. To do so will cause tension in the abdominal and surrounding muscles, and tension is what we're trying to avoid. Breathe no more than about 70% of your capacity. At the moment, if you're like most people you are only using about 20–30% of your lung capacity anyway, so 70% is a huge improvement. This 70% rule applies to all the other exercises as well.

Finding your diaphragm exercise

The aim of this exercise is to start mobilising the whole abdominal area. This will help loosen up the diaphragm and also help bring fresh blood to the digestive system and massage the internal organs. This helps enormously with problems such as constipation as it helps get things moving again. As with all breathing exercises, don't attempt to do so on a full stomach.

1. Ensure your lungs are relaxed (about half full). Bend forward at the waist, bend your knees slightly and place your hands on them. This will give you a stable position and allow gravity to help loosen the abdominal area.

2. Relax your stomach, allowing it to hang down under the pull of gravity.

3. Without breathing, pull your stomach in towards your spine and upwards slightly under your ribcage. Then push it down again to full distension. Keep pulling it in and pushing it down slowly and smoothly until you need to take a breath.

4. Take a few nice slow deep breaths to stabilise your breathing then bend forward and try again. Your aim is to try to feel the upward and downward movement of the diaphragm itself. Eventually you will be able to isolate its movement which will be of great help to your breath development.

If at any stage you start to feel light-headed then stop immediately and return to your normal breathing. However, don't give up the practice because the light-headed feeling indicates that your brain has taken in more oxygen than it is used to receiving. Take a break for a while then continue later and soon the feelings of dizziness will go as your cells get used to a higher level of oxygen.

The next exercise is called 'Sinking your breath' and success in this exercise is crucial. In fact, this whole book revolves around your ability to sink your breath. A lot of the postural points and exercises that are covered later rely on your ability to breathe into your centre of gravity, i.e. deep into your abdomen.

This exercise teaches you how to breathe in the most efficient manner. It uses all the correct muscles for breathing and so enables a full and effortless breath. The diaphragm, as it pulls down, draws air into the lungs and as it relaxes it moves back up again, but this action only partially empties the lungs. To empty them more fully requires the use of another set of muscles – your abdominals. For a long time now they have been a favourite target of fitness routines and magazine articles. However, one of their principal uses is in enabling a fuller exhalation.

Sinking your breath

1. Stand up straight, with your weight equally balanced between your feet.

2. Place your hands on your lower stomach with your thumbs in line with your navel. This will help you to feel the movement of your breath.

3. Imagine there is a balloon under your hands, deep in your stomach area, and breathe into it.

4. On the exhale, let your stomach relax back inwards then use your abdominal muscles to gently squeeze more air out. Pull your stomach in and up slightly as you did in the previous exercise. Don't forget the 70% rule here.

5. Focus on feeling and increasing the movement of your stomach under your hands. Let each breath be soft, smooth and slow. These are the three Ss that apply to all breathing exercises: Soft, Smooth, Slow.

6. When you are comfortable breathing deep into your abdomen you can try slowing down your breathing. Ensure that each in breath takes the same length of time as the out breath. This ensures that your body remains in balance. You can count inside your head to gradually increase the breaths and ensure they are even. Do so very gradually, and on no account should you strain or fight the breath in any way. A longer and fuller breath will come with time and practice.

This exercise trains both your ability to take in a fuller breath by using the correct muscles and also your mental focus on keeping your mind occupied on one thing. As such, it is a form of meditation, and indeed all meditations start with bringing the mind to focus on one thing.

After having spent a few minutes on this exercise, you may notice some or all of the following: feeling light-headed (as mentioned above), increased energy (from the extra oxygen), or feeling very tired and/or relaxed. This comes from the exhalation, and we'll discuss this shortly.

You should have managed to feel your abdomen rising and falling as the diaphragm pressed down as you breathed in, pushing your belly out, then relaxed, allowing gravity to push your belly back in again. If you did, then you're ready to move on to the next exercise. If not, then keep practising finding your diaphragm until you can feel the movement of your belly rising and falling clearly.

In kung fu we refer to the abdomen as the *centre*, for it is the centre of gravity, the centre of power and the centre of energy. Breathing into your centre unifies the top and bottom halves of your body.

The three breaths

Again focus on your breathing. I want you to time your in breaths and out breaths to see which is longer, if either. There are clearly three possibilities. A longer inhalation, a longer exhalation or a balanced breath where inhalation and exhalation are the same length.

Breathing has been found to be about so much more than just oxygen/CO_2 exchange. Each inhalation energises the body and each exhalation relaxes and releases tensions and toxins. This will help you to understand the three breaths, understand how your breathing habits may be contributing to your pain, energy levels and tension, and give you a long-term focus as well as short-term tricks to improve your everyday existence.

Inhaler breathers emphasise inhalation over exhalation. When done as a habit it brings in lots of energy but doesn't allow for a relaxing exhalation. Inhaler people tend to be highly stressed, nervous and on edge. They are more likely to be holding on to physical pain and may suffer from tension-related problems. IBS, constipation and other digestive upsets may plague them. The majority of people fall into this category, certainly the majority of pain-sufferers do.

One of the worst I've come across was a lady who had suffered temporomandibular joint disorder for some years. She had seen many specialists but jaw pain, almost constant headaches and dental problems persisted. One of the first things I noticed was that she never seemed to breathe out deeply. I taught her to balance her breathing and gave her local expansion exercises for her jaw area. Three months later, she was doing well, with most of her symptoms reduced or gone altogether.

Perhaps the one thing that distinguishes inhaler people is that they have an almost pathological unwillingness to let go. Performing a full exhalation feels like they have to let go of a lot of tensions, suppressed emotions and other stuff that feels very scary to them.

Exhaler breathers: These emphasise exhalation over inhalation. As such, they don't take in much oxygen or energy. They tend to be depressive, have low energy, are prone to colds and other infections, and often have cold hands and feet. Their lack of energy is likely to make them underachievers.

Balanced breathers: People whose in breaths match the depth and duration of their out breaths will be more balanced physically and mentally. They are at an excellent starting point for further breath development. However, even if your breath is balanced it is still likely to be constricted with tensions. These tensions will make you breathe inefficiently, into the wrong places.

Even people with balanced breathing may find times during their day when they are either too tense or too fatigued.

When this happens you can use either a prolonged inhalation to give you energy or a prolonged exhalation to breathe away the tensions. Here's how...

The turbo breath

When you are feeling tired and low in energy then do the turbo breath.

1. Exhale quickly and fully through your mouth as if you were saying 'ha' without vocalising it.

2. Breathe in slowly and fully through the nose.

3. Repeat as necessary.

The deflator breath

When you are feeling tense, anxious or stressed, then try this exercise.

1. Inhale quickly and fully through your nose.

2. Breathe out slowly and fully as if gently blowing on a candle flame, trying to move it without putting it out. As you exhale, relax your whole body downwards. Imagine you are a balloon that is being deflated; let yourself go limp and relaxed.

3. Repeat as necessary.

The three Ss

There are three qualities that we look for in a healthy breath and they all begin with the letter S. A good breath should be soft, slow and smooth.

Soft

Each breath should be soft, not forced in any way. It should require the minimum of effort to attain. You should feel as if you are being breathed rather than doing the breathing yourself.

Slow

You should aim to gradually slow down your breathing rate. Allow the same amount of time for the inhalation and the exhalation. You can do this by simply counting at a measured pace and gradually increase the numbers for each stage of the breath. For example, you may initially count to four for the in breath then another four for the out breath. After a few minutes this can go up to five, six or beyond. You will find that the process of focusing on and slowing down your breathing is very relaxing indeed.

Smooth

Each breath should be as smooth as possible. It should have no raggedy ends. If this happens, it means you are trying to breathe in or out too much: remember the 70% rule. The air should travel in and out of your lungs at the same speed. Smoothness of breath actually seems to smooth out your emotions and thought processes. Life suddenly seems so much easier.

The next exercise builds on the expansion principle introduced in the last chapter. Remember that we use expansion to counter the habitual and subconscious contractions of our muscles. In this exercise, you use your breathing to expand and open up your body, which is more powerful than using your mind alone.

The expansion breath

1. Start with abdominal breathing (see the Sinking your breath exercise above).

2. As you breathe in, feel that the air is expanding in all directions – up, down, sideways plus forward and backwards. Your breath is gradually filling up and compressing and supporting from the inside all your bones, muscles and organs. Gradually allow your breath to encompass as much of your body as possible, from your feet to the top of your head to your fingertips. This may sound strange, as you know you can't involve your legs, for example, in the breathing process but persevere with it and you may be amazed at the results. Your aim is to connect the whole of yourself together internally, gently expanding and compressing to the rhythm of your breathing.

3. As you exhale, maintain that same inner feeling of expansion and openness that your inhalation gave you, while releasing tension and relaxing everything downwards.

4. On the next inhale, expand and compress a little more.

With each inhalation and exhalation you are gradually opening up different parts of yourself to your breath and, in so doing, expanding your internal parts away from each other. At the same time, you are also using the compression of the breath to connect the different parts of yourself together in the same way that an inflatable rubber ring is internally connected. Later on, you will use this same expansion breath to help with your posture and also to increase your joint flexibility.

Hello hiccups – and goodbye

Finally, let's leave this chapter on breathing with what I consider to be the world's only working cure for hiccups. Getting hiccups can be a nightmare, as there seems to be no way of controlling them. Well, now there is – and it's another breathing exercise.

The technique is simple. You push the hiccups back down the body with your breath. When hiccups occur, breathe in then focus on your out breath.

The hiccup cure

1. Breathe in quickly then, as you exhale, empty your chest first.

2. When the chest is emptied, contract around the solar plexus area, then continue to contract and breathe out in the lower abdomen.

3. Mentally push down your hiccups by breathing out from the top and imagining the hiccups being pushed downwards.

4. breathe in quickly again and repeat.

Usually I can control them very quickly – within three or four hiccups. Occasionally they persist a little longer, but not much.

Peter realised that his breathing pattern was probably contributing to his fatigue and low moods. He focused on gradually slowing down and increasing his intakes of breath. He struggled to open up his centre, but then started to make progress. His energy started to pick up straight away but quickly went away again as his old habitual way of breathing kept reasserting itself. However, he did feel the benefits and so practised regularly. He started to regain his old vitality and once again started to look for work more seriously.

Janet was scared by her panic attack, and sought more information about it. She realised that short, shallow breathing was a major reason for her attack. She also sought to open up her abdomen and learn to breathe into her centre. This proved far more difficult than she had realised, as the tensions down there were holding on too strongly. So she started to open up her chest and gradually work her way downwards. Her breathing slowed down and became fuller, and she learned to exhale slowly and breathe out her troubles. Within a couple of weeks she felt more in control of herself and particularly her reactions to stress. She is still working on opening up her centre and is making progress every day.

A summary of Chapter 4

Your breathing habits have gradually changed over the course of your life. It is highly likely that core tensions are interfering with your ability to take a full, natural breath. Your current, poor breathing habits may be affecting your physical, emotional and mental health.

Every inhalation brings in oxygen, energy, resources and so on. If you feel tired, check your breathing and focus on longer, slower inhalations.

Every exhalation releases CO_2 as well as other toxins, and also helps release pent-up emotions. Most importantly, it also helps to release tension. If you are feeling tense you are almost certainly holding a lot of your breath in. Focus on long, slow exhalations.

Learn to breathe deep into your abdomen. This will greatly improve your breathing efficiency, help you to relax and improve your general health, particularly that of your digestive system.

If you get hiccups, push them down and out by breathing out from the chest first, then the middle of the body and finally the lower abdomen.

CHAPTER 5

The Posture of Stress

In this chapter:

> Why are postural problems so prevalent?
>
> Why is sitting down so bad for me?
>
> What does my posture say about my life?

Stress leads to tension and tension is stored in your posture. Every muscle that is more tense than it needs to be is affecting your skeleton, distorting your posture, lifting your bones up away from the ground and eating away at your energy. Every moment of every day, including when you're asleep, you are holding tightly on to tensions that are quite unnecessary. This chapter takes a look at the common postures of stress to see what damage they do, how and why we have acquired them, and what they can tell us about ourselves. It includes a marvellous exercise called 'the dragon's back'. This exercise mobilises the spine. It releases tension around the spine and also tone the core muscles. As if this wasn't enough, it also gives a good massage to the digestive organs to keep them toned and working efficiently. In the Jade Dragon system it is usually twinned with another exercise called 'the snake's back' which I'll teach in the next chapter.

You may be tempted to skip this chapter, believing that your posture is fine. I would be very surprised indeed if it is. Almost everyone, and I'm including myself here, has postural imbalances of one kind or another, and even the slightest of these can play havoc with your stress levels, health, balance, movements and energy levels.

Standing upright

Ever since man learned to stand on his two back legs he has had problems with his posture. Our transition from four-legged ape to one that moves solely on its two legs took a long time, about three to four million years. During that time our back legs became much stronger than our arms, although we still spent a lot of time climbing trees. Our hips narrowed to support the weight of our upper body, and we developed the natural curves of the spine and arches of the feet that helped absorb the shock of walking and running. Our thigh bones lengthened, which enabled us to take longer strides when walking or running, so that we could travel further and faster, and our knee joints strengthened to enable us to rest all our weight on one leg for walking.

There are many advantages to walking on two legs. It is easier to reach for and pick food from branches, it leaves the hands free to carry implements, weapons, babies etc., it makes us appear larger and more intimidating, and it enabled us to move quickly and change direction much faster than any four-legged animal can.

Interestingly, it is believed that the changes in our hips caused females' birth canal to narrow. This meant that women had to give birth much earlier than other primates, so early that our offspring are completely defenceless. This has created an imperative for a woman to find a mate who can not only impregnate her but will stick around throughout the pregnancy and for a long time afterwards to help look after the infant. Women have evolved to find stability in a relationship, while men are still following the old programming of spreading their seed as widely as possible to ensure the continuation of the species!

The advantages of being a biped are many, but they do come at a cost and that cost is often pain and limited movement. The spine in four-legged animals acts as an arch, with bones and organs hanging down from it. However, our spines act as a weight-bearing column. To enable it to bear weight efficiently and to withstand shocks, it developed an S-shaped curve. In many modern humans, the springiness of those graceful and useful curves has been severely diminished because of the high levels of tension in the back muscles. The back is no longer acting as an integral part of the whole walking/running structure and may be much less mobile and flexible. Shortly, we will be looking at a powerful exercise, the dragon's back, that will help to restore spinal mobility and so help prevent the back problems by which so many people are plagued.

It is in the lower back where the pressure is greatest that the back is most likely to be damaged. Under extreme pressure the discs between the vertebrae can pop out or become dislodged and press against spinal nerves. It seems that we humans are the only species that suffer from such back problems. Fortunately, it doesn't have to be that way.

We saw in Chapter 2 that there is an eternal tug of war going on in each of us. Opposing muscle groups pull on joints from both sides to try to maintain a status quo. However, sometimes one of these teams gets the upper hand and the joint or joints is moved almost permanently. If the muscles in the chest become too tense for the muscles in the upper back to compensate, then the shoulders will be pulled forward and the back will become rounded. Any attempt to try and force the body back into a balanced position can only exacerbate the problem as it will put even more strain on the muscles and tendons that control the upper part of the body. The only real answer is to release the tension in the chest to open up the joints and allow the body to regain its previous balance. As a general rule, wherever you see a curve in someone's posture, then the muscles on the inside of the curve are too tight and need releasing, and the muscles on the outside aren't strong enough to straighten out the curve. It's always better to release the tension on the inside of the curve than strengthen the muscles on the outside as that will just add to the tug of war.

Few people, if any, have a perfectly symmetrical posture.

If you study someone closely, you will very likely notice that one shoulder is slightly higher than the other or one side of the neck is shorter or the head is tilted to one side and so on. Less noticeable but equally common are imbalances in the hip area, differing leg length and, of course, spinal abnormalities. We tend to only notice these when they become very pronounced but a greater awareness of your own posture. Following the advice in this book can prevent you from ending up with these issues.

Kyphosis, Lordosis and Scoliosis

There are three common spinal abnormalities and these are known as kyphosis, lordosis and scoliosis.

Kyphosis

Kyphosis is the rolling forward of the upper back which causes a hunchback. The shoulders appeared curved and the scapulas are positioned further away from the spine. This condition is characterised by excessive tightness in the chest area. The chest is sunken and closed and the head, shoulders and back fold around it. Kyphosis can be caused by many factors, including degenerative diseases, injuries, muscular conditions, slipped discs and, often, a change in posture/routine, from habitually carrying a heavy bag to a change in job or sleeping position. Most often, though, it is simply due to excess tightness in the muscles of the front of the body. I foresee that incidences of kyphosis will become far more common in the future as we spend more time slumping in chairs, with the front of the body compressed, and leaning out head and body forward to stare at TV and computer screens. Most jobs now involve sitting at computers or behind a steering wheel and so we spend increasingly long periods of time immobile and hunched into positions that make kyphosis more likely.

Kyphosis often leads to pain from the vastly overused chest muscles, tiredness from the strain of having to hold on to that tension and, in some cases, breathing problems as the chest wall is not open as it should be. The head protrudes forward, which severely affects balance, as it is no longer over the feet. The muscles all along the back and the back of the neck have been pulled incredibly tight by the pressure from the chest muscles. Deep tissue massage is required to release the incredible tension in these muscles. Skeletal realignment by a chiropractor or an osteopath may be necessary as well, but the tension must be released first. After all this, the body must be retrained to prevent these tensions building up again. Individuals tending towards kyphosis should emphasise stretching movements that stretch the front of the body, particularly the muscles of the abdomen, chest, front of shoulders and front and sides of neck – see Chapter 8 on flexibility for more information.

Lordosis

While kyphosis is caused by tension in the chest pulling the upper back forward, lordosis is caused by tension in the lower back arching the lower spine backwards. The abdominal muscles that should oppose the movement aren't strong enough to resist the high levels of tension and prevent an inward curve in the central lower back. This excessive curvature of the lower back can make the belly protrude, which is not a look many people want these days!

It is believed that if the spine is flexible and the curve can be straightened by bending forward, then there is no need to seek help. This may not be helpful advice, as the tension in the lower back needs to be released as it can lead to low back pain and potentially to a back injury. Once again, the answer is to release the tension in the lower back through deep tissue massage. Then, stretching of the lower back, added to strengthening of the core abdominal muscles, should correct the problem. Individuals tending towards lordosis should emphasise stretching movements that bend the body forward at the waist - see Chapter 8 on flexibility.

Kyphosis and lordosis represent an exaggerated curve of the normal and natural curves of the spine. As I mentioned earlier, these curves are there to help absorb the shocks of walking and running but the fact that we have these curves means that there is the risk of the curves becoming abnormally pronounced.

Scoliosis

There is nothing natural about the curve of scoliosis. It is a lateral curve or S shape that runs left to right or right to left. Scoliosis can go unnoticed by many unless it's particularly pronounced or you know what to look for. Scoliosis is more difficult to treat than the other problems mentioned above but, again, massage followed by osteopathy or chiropractic is recommended. The snake's back exercise, presented later, is also of great help to individuals with scoliosis.

There was quite a bit of theory in this section for you to read, so I think it's time you stood up and did something! Here is a great exercise for mobilising the spine, both front and back. It tones the core muscles of the centre and opens and loosens the muscles that support the spine. The release of tension that this exercise brings can dramatically improve your flexibility but, of course, as with all exercises it needs to be practised regularly to gain the benefits.

Dragon's back exercise

1. Stand with your feet about hip-width apart, feet facing forward and knees slightly bent.

2. Tilt your hips forward, sticking your bottom out. Then bend your knees, tilt your hips back again and straighten your knees more. Your tailbone should be drawing a circle going back, down, forward then up again.

3. Continue the movement for 20–30 seconds and gradually increase the time.

4. As you continue the movement, aim to gradually release the tension in your spine; feel the area opening up and allowing movement through. Gradually, as the tension in your back muscles releases, you will feel a wave of movement going up your spine. To start with, the movement may feel a bit jerky but, with practice, the muscles surrounding the spine open up and the whole body moves in a sinuously wavy pattern that goes from the hips all the way up to the head and down into the feet. When you can achieve this, you have made the dragon's back.

5. If you wish, you can add arm movement. Raise them above your head as you did in the arm hang exercise. Let their weight push your shoulder blades down, then begin the dragon's back exercise. Allow the wave that comes up from your centre to go up through your shoulders, elbows and wrists and out to your fingers.

This simple exercise produces more flexibility in the intervertebral joints as well as the muscles that support the spine, which enable the spine to perform its role of absorbing the impact of walking and running.

Let's divert our attention briefly and take a look at one of the biggest enemies of good posture – the chair.

The unergonomic chair

Humans have been sitting down for a very long time. Chairs were recorded in ancient Egypt at least 5000 years ago, but it wasn't until the sixteenth century that chairs became commonplace in the Western world.

Millions of years of evolution have led to our bones being stacked on top of each other in a certain way, but chairs put the human body in unnatural positions that stress areas that aren't used to it. The unnatural act of sitting on chairs chronically shortens the muscles of the hamstrings, hip flexors and other muscles, and weakens the muscles that oppose them and which could provide a balance. Sitting down weakens the legs in general, which causes tension to accumulate in the abdomen, chest and back to lift the weight of the upper body away from the weakened legs. The body spends many hours in this unnatural position, with much of its weight resting on the lumbar curve which wasn't designed for this.

Despite the current trend for ergonomic chairs, no chair is good for your posture.

There is one simple piece of advice I can give you regarding chair use, apart from limiting the amount of time you spend sitting on them, and that is to at least limit the amount of damage that chair use will do to you. The advice is this. Use the back of your chair for hanging your coat on and nothing else. In other words, don't lean back on the chair back. Learn to use the postural muscles in your back and abdomen to maintain an upright position. Most chairs enable you to do this, although sofas are particularly deadly. That's why I spend more time sitting on the floor than I do on our sofa.

Before chairs were invented, man used the traditional resting postures of squatting, cross-legged sitting or kneeling, all of which were able to maintain the integrity and flexibility of posture. Squatting is particularly beneficial. Man, like his fellow primates, has always used the squatting position for resting, working and performing bodily functions. Infants from every culture instinctively squat to relieve themselves, to rest and to play with items on the floor. Most adults lack the flexibility in the calf and gluteal muscles and strength in the core muscles to be able to squat effectively. The gluts are

81

another key muscle group that suffers badly from chair use. The dragon's back exercise is one way of helping to regain a healthy squatting posture, although flexibility exercises working on other joints are also essential if you are again to squat comfortably.

Your postural map

'As any action or posture, long continued, will distort and disfigure the limbs; so the mind likewise is crippled and contracted by perpetual application to the same set of ideas. It is easy to guess the trade of an artisan by his knees, his fingers, or his shoulders: and there are few among men of the more liberal professions, whose minds do not carry the brand of their calling, or whose conversation does not quickly discover to what class of the community they belong.'
(Samuel Johnson, 1751)

Everybody's posture changes and evolves throughout their life. We are born without undue tension and in our early childhood delight in the free movement and boundless energy that this lack of tension gives. However, soon children learn to sit on chairs and watch TV, and the rot sets in. I was quite disturbed the other day to note that my five-year-old daughter could no longer touch her toes while keeping her knees straight. As a baby she used to giggle as we held one leg down then bent the other one up to touch her nose! Within a few short years, much of that flexibility has already gone. As she becomes older, so her posture will gradually change and those changes will depend on many factors, including but not limited to the following.

Day-to-day activities, including work

Clearly, how you use your body plays a major role in how your posture develops. People who spend a lot of the day sitting in front of a computer or behind a steering wheel are more likely to develop kyphosis as the lower back is slumped, the upper back is raised and the head is pushed forward. People who habitually carry a heavy bag over one shoulder will develop more musculature on one side than the other. This can compensate all the way down the spine, potentially leading to scoliosis. Those who spend a lot of time standing up and leaning forward will develop tension in the lower back muscles, which can lead to lordosis in later life.

Any position or habitual movement you spend a lot of time in, including your sleeping positions, will have an influence on your posture.

History of illness and injury

Any period of illness where you are bed-bound will weaken you considerably. In fact, just two weeks spent in bed can make you too weak to be able to stand up and move around – the muscle loss is that quick. How you regain your strength after an illness is critical. Good physiotherapy is essential, to ensure that a wide range of movement is regained, to ensure that a balanced musculature is redeveloped and a return to good posture can be achieved.

Injuries can also have a serious effect on posture. When you injure yourself, tension instantly develops around the site of injury to prevent further movement and thus worsening the injury. The more severe the injury, the tighter and more widespread is the tension, and this adds significantly to the pain and the recovery time afterwards. One of the roles of a physiotherapist is to release this tension using deep tissue massage and ultrasound. If this tension is left untreated it can linger for years, causing pain, limited movement and increasing the risk of injuring the area again. An expert physical therapist can diagnose quite precisely where a person has previously injured themselves just by looking at their posture. For example, if the left calf muscles were thicker than the right, this could indicate an injury in the right leg and the left leg bearing more weight to compensate. This compensation would affect the hips and from there up the spine, and the therapist would find more tension in the muscles on the right side of the spine than the left, and so on. The body will always try to compensate as best it can for whatever tensions it's holding on to in relation to whatever postures or movements we demand of it.

Role models: parents, peers and people of special significance

As we grow up, we subconsciously model people we emulate. A young girl's biggest influence is her mother, so she will subconsciously copy the way she walks, her mannerisms and speech patterns. I sometimes find myself mirroring some of my dad's mannerisms even now. As she grows she may, more consciously, copy some of her friends or celebrities that she likes. Again these can become hardwired into her posture.

Moods and emotions

I'm sure most people are aware of a link between your mood and your posture. Depressed people have a collapsed posture, with shoulders slumped forward, head down, chest collapsed onto the midriff and so on. This posture is lifeless and limp and barely allows them to breathe. The posture is caused by their depressed mood, but it's important to remember that as long as they maintain the posture it will be very difficult for them to come out of their depression. At the other end of the scale, a happy person is full of life and vigour. They are bursting with energy and you can almost see it itching to escape from every joint. The eyes are alive, the hands expressive and each step has more springiness than a trampoline. Again, this alive and alert posture adds to their feeling of wellbeing. Examples abound of emotions being expressed through posture – a person with too much responsibility carrying their shoulders too high, a proud and egotistical man with his chest inflated, and so on. This link between posture, breath and emotions could fill a whole book – and indeed, it is the book I plan to write next.

What's happening right now

Suddenly had a shock? Feeling tired? Have a pain somewhere? It doesn't take any special expertise to recognise when something out of the ordinary and unexpected happens to someone, as their posture and facial expressions will often signpost what's going on. These 'postures of now', as I call them, will override your 'mood posture' – though it's interesting to note that the way you react will usually follow the same lines as the reactions of your parents, peers or people of special significance. They will be modified slightly to fit in with your 'occupational and health posture', but will be largely modelled on others all the same. It would be interesting to know how far back this modelling goes. Are we imitating the mannerisms of our great-great-grandparents without even knowing it?

Your posture reflects the person you are now.

Your posture reflects the bumps and knocks you've had in your life, it gives clues to your profession and how you spend your leisure and sleeping time, it mirrors the actions of those who have been important in your life, and it gives away your emotions, feelings and responses to what's going on around you. Your 'occupational and health posture' is your default and, to a large extent, your identity. It is often modified by your 'mood posture', which can be quickly overridden by a 'posture of now'. However, the 'occupational and health posture' won't really change at all – at least, not without some significant work on your part. The rest of this book discusses the work you would have to do to change this.

Layers of armour

As I have mentioned, there are reasons why tension was created and part of that is to give us a physical armour to mirror the psychological armouring that happens in our mind when we feel under threat. If you see someone prowling around outside your house one night, probably the first thing you'll be concerned about is improving the security of your home with window locks, extra bolts, deadlocks and so on. Even if you don't see anyone else prowling around for years, the memory of how you felt seeing someone sneaking around your garden will ensure that you keep the extra security in place. Our minds and bodies are like this. When they feel threatened they take precautions with mental and physical armouring that helps us to feel a measure of security. The physical armouring is the layers of tension that tie up our muscles. The mental armouring has to do with the way we relate to other people. Our ability to be caring and sensitive towards others diminishes as a way of ensuring that, if they hurt us – well, we didn't care about them anyway. Our sensitivity towards them as a fellow member of the human race lessens and so we can treat others without regard for their feelings.

The physical armouring of our bodies starts when we are very young – some say even in the womb. As an infant we have no personal power, and must rely on our parents or carers for our every need. Our needs at that age are few: warmth, shelter, milk and a clean nappy are what we need physically. However, we have another need which is just as important, which is physical contact, and lots of it. Generally, this contact comes from being held by parents. There has been much research that clearly shows that babies who spend a lot of time 'in arms' grow up to have a more balanced personality, a stronger sense of self and fewer emotional traumas and disturbances. Children who are deprived of the regular loving touch of parents or carers learn early on that they are unloved and must fend for themselves. The physical and mental armouring starts and they either show less concern for their fellow children or compensate by becoming over-generous towards others.

You can look at this from the point of view of energy fields. When a mother gives her daughter her direct attention, she is giving her energy. When she holds her in her arms, she is merging her own energy field with that of her daughter, and so the child feels safe in her mother's strong and loving energy. Until the child is able to survive on her own energy, she desperately needs to get energy from others around her in the form of physical contact or attention. Most of her time, in fact, is spent finding ways to get this contact and attention. She learns that certain words, noises, facial expressions and actions will give her attention, and so she focuses on these rather than the ones that get her ignored.

If a child is in need of energy and her actions are being ignored she will choose other actions that will get her noticed. These may well be actions that we consider 'naughty' but, for the child, any kind of attention, even if it provokes anger, is better than no attention at all. The quality of energy she gets depends on the mood of the person giving the energy. She is hoping for loving energy which feels smooth and warm and makes her feel good. The energy of anger is brittle and spiky and feels wrong and painful for her, and so she starts crying. The only real way to calm her down is to be calm yourself and give her the warm, loving energy she needs.

When her demands for energy are persistently ignored, she starts to realise that she won't get what she needs. She ceases to feel protected by others and so takes steps to protect herself. The physical armouring of her body tends to start in the region of the navel – the place where she was connected to her mother in the womb. This is most likely the place where all your earliest and deepest traumas will be stored. These traumas will have to do with your most fundamental beliefs about your identity and your place in the world, your ability to form friendships or romantic entanglements, your need to be controlling or passive, aggressive or just plain invisible, your attitude towards authority and many other such fundamental beliefs.

From the navel the tension spreads outwards, contracting the entire body inwards. It is this contraction that we need to learn to control and reverse.

Holding on to tension has become a habit, and one that is far more difficult to break than smoking. Whereas a smoker may smoke one cigarette per hour, you are holding on to tension all the time, twenty-four hours a day. Constant vigilance is required to release it as you will habitually acquire it again then need to consciously release it again, and so on.

Tension is more than just a habit. You acquired that tension for a reason and that reason may still exist although in many cases it may have ceased to exist a long time ago and is now purely habitual. So if an area that you're working on isn't responding as you'd hoped, there is probably an underlying reason for it. With enough sensitivity and patience, you may eventually get to the core of the problem and then you can deal with it, which will release that area of tension and probably a few of the surrounding areas as well. This is a journey, an almost constant battle to release existing layers of tension as well as the ones you have yet to form. During it, you should, I hope, learn to stop yourself from layering your body with the armour of physical tension.

The next chapters will teach you ways of sitting, standing, walking and moving that will help you to release some of that tension and to prevent it from building up so fast.

A summary of Chapter 5

Our status as a biped means we have to be able to balance various forces acting on our skeleton. Lacking the stability of four legs, we use specific tensions to hold us upright. Unfortunately, we often use the wrong muscles to keep us upright and balanced and so put constant, excess force on muscles that weren't designed for it.

The spine is at particular risk as it carries the weight of the upper body, including all its organs and muscles, and conveys that weight down through the hips into the legs. Any misalignment in the spine means that tension will develop elsewhere to prevent us from toppling over.

Your posture is a result of many forces, including your history of sickness and injury, your occupation, leisure interests, past and present emotional states and parental/peer modelling.

Much of your tension is no more than a habitual way of holding yourself. It really isn't necessary. So all you need to do is to learn more efficient ways of carrying yourself.

Always remember that your body is highly adaptable. Unfortunately it has adapted itself to the many hours you have spent locked in unhealthy positions. To maintain those positions with the greatest ease it has created tension and lots of it that keeps you locked in the positions that you clearly favour.

CHAPTER 6

The Stress-Proof Posture

In this chapter

> How can I learn not to hold on to tension all the time? What
> are the three things I need to remember when I'm standing or
> sitting?

> My shoulders often seem to be tight and raised up when I'm
> stressed. Is my posture at fault?

This chapter will tell you what you need to know to develop a posture that
doesn't hold on to tension. Follow the principles outlined here and eventually
the everyday stresses of your life will be as water off a duck's back. I know
this is so, because your mind and your body are mirror images of each other.
If you are stressed you will create tension in your posture. If you consciously
prevent that from happening, then the stress you feel is reduced dramatically
until it almost vanishes. With such a small stress response it means your mind
and body can find the most appropriate way to act. You will act consciously
rather than react blindly as you once did.

Your stress-proof posture is one that is aligned with gravity and holds on
to only the smallest amount of tension necessary. Thus it allows full, natural,
efficient and effortless movement. It is one that also allows fluidity,
springiness, grace and a sense of aliveness in all you do. This chapter is here to
help you achieve this posture. It will take some time to make the necessary
adjustments, but remember that your posture is one that will last the rest of
your life. In fact it, quite literally, carries you through your life. So I believe it
is worth spending a little bit of time working on developing a posture that is
stress-proof, efficient and will serve you well for decades to come.

There are many benefits to improving your posture. Here are the main
ones. You will:

> learn how to release tension, at any time, anywhere

be able to maintain a healthy posture and alignments well into your old age

avoid the common spinal imbalances of kyphosis, lordosis and scoliosis

improve your balance and natural grace

be better able to deal with stressful situations.

A perfect posture is one that is aligned with gravity and is able to move freely while holding on to just enough tension to keep itself upright. This means it uses very little energy to maintain and so has plenty of energy in reserve. Tension isn't keeping muscles unnecessarily contracted, and so there is a lot of strength held in reserve for when it's needed. Just like a cat, the body is held very relaxed for most of the time but is capable of huge levels of power and grace when necessary. When a stressful situation occurs, the mind and body deal with the crisis and then, crucially, release the unneeded tension; there is a distinct letting go so that the person can then move on to enjoy life freely – until the next mini crisis.

The four requirements of good posture

In order to achieve this posture – what I call the stress-proof posture – four things need to occur:

1. Your legs need to become stronger.

2. Your body must be fully aligned with gravity.

3. You need to learn to stabilise yourself effectively.

4. Your body must be allowed to relax downwards.

Let's look at these in more detail.

1. Your legs need to become stronger

Tension in the upper body is often a constant companion because most people's legs are too weak to be able to support their upper frame effectively.

Muscle mass is lost very quickly when you don't exercise, as it is impossible for your body to maintain powerful muscles when they aren't being used. The leg and hip muscles can, and often do, become so weak that they are no longer able to carry the weight of the upper body effectively. So tension is maintained in the hips, shoulders and so on, to take the strain off the legs. Even if you do have stronger legs through exercise, you are likely to be maintaining tension in the upper body as that is your habitual way of holding yourself. As you now know, this is made even worse when you become stressed.

Your first goal should be to strengthen your legs. This is done easily, by standing with your feet facing forward and your knees bent. This will ensure that your weight is over your knee joints properly and won't damage your knees. When you can do this comfortably for a minute or so, then widen your stance more and bend your knees further. It also helps to slowly move your weight from one leg to the other, but remember to keep your body upright (see the point below).

2. Your body must be fully aligned with gravity

Ever since we first stood upright to gain mobility and to free up our hands to manipulate tools and food, we have been struggling to maintain our upright posture. The human skeleton is perfectly capable of standing upright and maintaining that posture throughout its life. Chapter 5 explained why most of us end our days bent over and barely able to move, unbalanced and robbed of energy. What I didn't describe then is that, when the body stops being aligned with gravity, it requires constant tension to prevent you from falling over. When aligned properly, everything is stacked on top of each other; the head over the spine, over the, hips, over the feet, etc. Very little tension is required to keep it that way.

The only way to be relaxed and relatively free of tension is to be upright, aligned with the constant down-force of gravity.

When you are upright and balanced, everything feels easier. You can walk more quickly, change direction more easily, pick things up more easily and so on. All of these things and more become more efficient and easier to do. As you saw in Chapter 5, your posture has a large part to play in your . A balanced posture leads to a balanced and neutral mood, which is the ideal state for most things in life. If you are bent forward, weighed down by your own posture, then you will feel as if you have the cares of the world on your shoulders. This is bound to affect your emotional state just as your emotions will affect your posture. There is nothing wrong with emotions, as long as you recognise how they pull your posture, energy levels and mental processes in different directions.

One of the most important aspects of your whole posture is learning to maintain a part of your focus on your feet. I'm sure that most of the time you're walking around with scarcely a thought for your poor, overused and under appreciated feet. They carry you through your life and unless they start aching ie shouting loudly at you that enough is enough then you barely consider them. You should start doing so now for three very good reasons:

1. Keeping your attention on your feet dramatically improves your balance and stability particularly when walking on uneven ground or times when you may need to be balanced on one leg. Maintaining alignment with gravity will be so much easier when your mind knows precisely where your feet are and what is under them.

2. Keeping some attention on the feet prevents you from tensing up so much when under pressure. Your muscles tend to flow in a wave towards wherever your attention is. When stressed the attention rises to the head and the muscles follow suit. When you have a stomach ache, your attention goes there and the muscles contract inwards and so on. Keep your attention on your feet, or at least part of it and the muscles will flow downward and the only way they can do that is by releasing tension.

3. In order for your brain to feel a part of your body it must increase the neural pathways between itself and the part to be felt. The best way for it to do this is to release the tensions that may be interfering with those pathways. Hence by focusing on a part of the body you will gain some release of tension in the area and all the way up to the head.

Align yourself with gravity exercise

1. Stand upright with your feet about shoulder-width apart and with the knees bent slightly.

2. Your feet should be facing forward as much as possible to reduce stress on your knee joints. The feet should be flat on the floor, with your weight spread evenly across their width.

3. Look straight ahead. Looking down will tilt your head forward and lead to tension all down your neck and back. Lift the top of your head and gently pull back the back of your head to prevent it moving forwards. It can help to imagine you have a face on the back of your head.

4. Rock yourself forwards and backwards on your feet until you find the central point that feels balanced.

5. Remain standing in that position for a minute or so more, remaining conscious of your feet and your balance.

6. Now try tilting your head forward slightly. If you have remained balanced, you should feel your whole body being pulled forward by the weight of your head. Now try tilting it slightly backwards for the same effect.

7. Move your weight slowly to left and right and also backwards and forwards onto the heels and balls of the feet, until your weight is perfectly aligned downward through the very centre of your feet. Don't allow your knees to collapse inwards, as this will bring your weight on to the insides of your feet and also misalign your knee joints. Keep looking straight forward.

With practice, you will become more aware of your physical balance and alignment at all times. You will feel how the tension levels in your body change when you are forced to move in an unbalanced way. You will become more sure-footed and, because you are balanced, you will require less tension in every move you make. It is important, so do find the time to practice it.

3. You need to learn to stabilise yourself more efficiently

Learning to use different muscles to hold yourself up gives you instant, powerful relaxation.

Most people are surprised to discover that there is more than one way to hold yourself in any position. The way you hold yourself and move your body have become such ingrained habits that it's hard to imagine there could be another, better way.

Different muscles in your body have different roles to play. This is fairly obvious, but what's less well understood by most people is that the muscles nearest the surface of the body are designed to move the skeleton, i.e. you, around. These are our mobilisers and, in order to be able to move freely, they should be as free of tension as possible. We have another set of muscles, deeper inside and closer to the skeleton itself, that are not designed to move joints but to stabilise the skeleton. The stabilisers, as they are known, are slow twitch muscles which means they are very efficient at burning oxygen slowly and so can maintain a continuous contraction over a long period of time. The soleus muscles in your calves will be mostly of this type, to enable you to stand for long periods of time without them failing. Your mobilisers are fast twitch muscles, designed to contract with enough strength and speed to move a joint *and then to relax again.* They aren't designed to maintain a degree of tension twenty-four hours a day. This is where a large part of your problem comes in as, if the muscles of movement are stiff with subconsciously held tension, then they can't do their jobs effectively. They will be constantly burning oxygen inefficiently and will become far more prone to the pain and injury of overuse.

Holding yourself in position using the wrong muscles will tire you out very quickly.

Many people end up using their mobilisers to stabilise their body, and this is partly because they are the muscles over which we have most direct control. The stabilisers tend to lie deep in the body and, because they don't really move the skeleton much, we have less conscious control over them and it is more difficult to feel when they are working.

So the obvious question is, how do we release the mobilisers and let the stabilisers take the strain? Well, the theory is simple but the practice less so.

All you need do is release any excess tension in any part of the body and let it sink downwards under the pull of gravity. The muscles you're able to release tension in will be your mobilisers, and you will usually feel a faint tightening up somewhere else. That should be a stabiliser kicking in to take up the workload.

The invisible stool and other stabilisers

As I mentioned, it is difficult enough to feel the stabilisers, let alone consciously contract them to stabilise the skeleton. It is much easier to create tension in our mobiliser muscles. Hence, it is very difficult to release that tension as we are aware that part of that tension is needed to keep us upright and maintain our posture. The good news is that, although you cannot consciously contract your stabilisers, you can trick them into working. This sounds a bit strange, but we can do this quite easily just by imagining that different parts of our body are resting on something. This is surprisingly powerful. Try it now.

However you are sitting or standing at the moment, bring your attention to your elbows and imagine that they are resting on something. This works whether your hands are resting on something or are in midair.

As you focus on them resting on a support of some kind, your shoulders will be tricked into thinking there is no longer a need for them to be tensing up to pull your elbows upwards. Immediately, or at least within seconds, you will feel tension in your shoulders dissolving and your shoulders sinking downwards. Sometimes this works better in the hands than the elbows. It depends on what position your arms are in. Mentally try it in both positions and see which works best. Soon you'll instinctively know where to place the mental stabilisers to best effect. Think how much less tiring typing on your keyboard will be from now on! That's a great way to practise this.

Another good place to try this is the head. Imagine your chin is resting comfortably on something, then feel what happens to your upper back and neck. What you are feeling is a reduction in the kyphotic curve as the top of your spine comes back into a more natural and healthy position. Don't overdo this to start with – ten seconds or so at a time will be enough. It may not feel like much is happening, but you may be amazed at the strength of the forces involved. Regularly practising this will open the front of your body, which is often overly contracted, and greatly improve your posture. You will stand and walk tall, graceful and proud.

There is more than one way for your body to hold any position. You habitually always use the same way but it may well not be the best way.

The next important one is the invisible stool. Imagine that there is a stool behind you. Bend your knees slightly and pretend to sit on this stool. This will change how your weight drops through your hips and knees and make you more stable in your movements.

The other main place to try this is in the feet. When you are standing, you naturally imagine that your feet are supporting your weight. You may, though, be surprised at how much of that weight is being lifted up by tension in the hips and upper body. When standing or walking, imagine that you're feet are encased in cement. The weight of this pulls them firmly down onto the ground. This will make your stance much more stable and balanced.

4. Relax downwards

The more relaxed downwards you are, the better is your connection to the earth and the more powerful you will feel.

When your body is being lifted up from above by excess tension, you feel unrooted, top heavy, prone to stress and weak. Learn to relax down, to connect yourself more firmly to the planet, and you will feel so much stronger and better able to cope with stress.

When your body is perfectly aligned with gravity then it requires only a bare minimum of tension in certain muscles to hold it in that position and to move it. The rest of your muscles should be able to relax downwards. When this happens the weight of the relaxed muscles pulls your skeleton down towards the earth. You feel heavier, more rooted, more connected to the planet. With this comes a feeling of self control and personal power. The more connected to the ground you are then the more powerful you will feel. This is one of the secrets used by many powerful and charismatic leaders.

Sounds great but if only it were as simple as just being able to relax you tension when you become aware of it. Unfortunately, this requires conscious attention and lots of it. As you now know about the tension paradox you know that you have no feedback mechanism to tell you when your muscles are fully relaxed and when they're still holding on to tension. Now that you have strengthened your legs, are aligned with gravity and are mentally stabilising yourself, what you need to do is drop your tensions downwards.

Much of our language seems to be subconsciously saying how we're really feeling. When we're stressed we 'tense up', when someone annoys us they 'get our back up'. These sayings are literally true. When you are under stress, your muscles contract and lift you up away from the ground. This tension lifts your body's weight away from your legs, which become weakened as a result. The two most common places where tension lifts you up the most is in the hips/waist area which, subconsciously, lift the legs, and in your shoulders, which lift and support your arms. Your arms and legs do not need to be constantly pulled upwards by the tension in your hips and shoulders but, as you were unaware until now that it's even happening, you were unable to stop it. The tension in the hips prevents your weight from dropping through the legs as it should, which weakens the legs and puts great strain on the hip area. The tension in your shoulders prevents full and powerful expression through the arms and causes tension in the upper back, neck and head. Your waist area acts like a nineteenth-century corset, lifting and supporting the upper body and pulling in any unsightly bulges in the waistline. The shoulders also raise up when you're under pressure, in an effort to pull up and stabilise the body from above. Now that you're aware of this tendency, you can counter it and relax down.

The four step relaxing down process

Learning to stand in a relaxed manner is best done as a four-step process.

1. Relax your centre down onto your feet.

2. Relax your head and arms down onto your centre.

3. Relax your head and arms all the way down to your feet.

4. Maintain that full-body relaxation while moving (see next chapter).

1. Relax your centre down onto your feet

You should try to focus on this every day. Relax your feet so you can feel the ground beneath your feet, and try to feel the weight of your centre being transferred directly into your feet. Within a short time it will feel right and you will quickly realise how different it feels from the usual way you use (or misuse) your legs. You will realise how heavy your upper body is when it drops down through your legs properly. The challenge is to maintain that feeling for as long as you can and, eventually, to make it your habitual way of standing. This will strengthen your legs very quickly and you will feel much more planted and stable than you have before.

Relax your hips

Your hips, like your shoulders, carry a lot of extra tension. This prevents you from dropping your weight down through your legs and into the ground, which makes you physically more stable. Excess tension in the hips can lead to lower back pain, constipation, sexual problems and much more. It further prevents freedom of movement in your legs and drains you of energy, as the large muscles of the hips are often locked up.

Again, your hips are constantly trying to lift your legs up away from the ground instead of acting as a channel to drop the weight of the upper body through them and down through the legs to root into the ground as they should. The answer to this is much the same as it was for your shoulders, only this time you should imagine a feeling of weight in the feet and lower legs up to the knees. Stand up and spend a few minutes focusing on dropping your knees downwards. This will have the dual effect of releasing tension in your hips and also more firmly rooting your feet into the ground. Be aware, though, that your hips and upper legs contain some of the strongest muscles in the body and are holding on to a lot of tension so it may be a while before you feel any appreciable benefit, or even notice much difference. Keep at it, though, as when you do feel the difference it will be very noticeable and will start to restore the natural springiness of your hips, legs and feet. So many people have lower bodies that are so stiff with tension that they have completely lost their natural grace and bounce.

It is a rare but pleasant sight to see the occasional person who can still use their hips and legs to walk properly.

If you want to see a graceful walk, go to Africa or search out videos of African women who have learned from a young age to balance loads on their heads. This has forced them to walk tall and to use their hips, knees and ankles to absorb the forces of walking on uneven ground and to maintain the top-heavy load over their centre of gravity. Many actors use the same technique by balancing books on their head. Perhaps you could try it too!

2. Relax your head and arms down onto your centre

To start with, your first priority should be to strengthen your legs and relax the upper body down to the feet. However, you can also start to work on relaxing your upper body. Keep your spine upright and allow all your other muscles and other soft tissues to relax down around the spine. Extend your arms in front of your body with the elbows relaxed down as far as they will go. This weight in your elbows will pull your shoulders down. Again, hold this position for as long as possible; several minutes at a time is best.

Release your shoulders

Tension in the neck and shoulders causes upper back pain, headaches, eye problems, a tendency to panic easily, an inability to deal with stress, insomnia and many other complaints. Excess shoulder tension is so common that I can state with confidence that you are suffering from it.

The reasons for this are, first, that the shoulder is the most mobile of all the joints. Over twenty separate muscles move each shoulder, so the chances of you using the shoulder joint inefficiently are far greater than, say, the elbow joint.

The second reason is that you, like virtually everyone else, are almost certainly using your shoulders to lift and support your arms. There seems to be an inbuilt fear in all of us that if we don't use our shoulders to lift our arms up then, somehow, they will fall off. Trust me, they won't. They are firmly attached with ligaments, tendons, muscles, fascia, skin and so on.

The answer to how to release shoulder tension and to prevent yourself from gaining yet more is to learn to use your arms differently. Instead of allowing your arms to be lifted up by your shoulders, imagine that your elbows are heavy and that weight is pulling your shoulders down. Try this now. Focus on your elbows and feel their weight. That weight should drag them down to a near-vertical position. This is a much healthier position than a more horizontal one, which maintains your shoulder tension. The trick, of course, is to incorporate this weighted-elbow feeling into your everyday life. When driving, drop your elbows down to prevent tension building up in the neck and shoulders. When using a computer, maintain an upright stance, don't lean towards the screen, and imagine your elbows are weighted down while typing.

One simple way to show how much tension is holding your arms and shoulders up is to sit in front of a table or desk and place your hands palm down on it. It may initially escape your attention, but very little of the weight in your arms and hands is now resting on the table. Most of it is being held up by tension in the shoulders and back. In fact, were you to rest the whole weight of your arms on the table then that weight should be enough to pull your hands off the table. Imagine your hands are glued to the table, and slowly release the tension in your neck, shoulders and back. Your elbows should be hanging down and should feel heavy. This feels unnatural, because you are so used to using excess tension to hold yourself up. Getting used to the feeling of being tension-free should be one of your main goals.

What feels natural to you is to be constantly holding yourself up with excess tension.

Your hips and shoulders are the two most difficult places to release tension from, as there are many, strong muscles involved, and the habits have been ingrained over a lifetime. However, although the path ahead of you may be long, every step of the way will relax more tension and release more energy into the bargain. Imagining and feeling extra weight in your elbows and knees will go a long way towards being able to let go of the tensions that are holding you up – and holding you back.

3. Relax your head and arms all the way down to your feet

If you have managed the last two points, then this should be a fairly easy transition. All it requires is for you to release the tension in the centre of your body to allow the weight of your upper body to drop straight down to your feet. You should feel a direct connection between your feet and your head. The other vital connection is between your feet and your hands. Any time you try to push, pull or lift something, you need to be feeling the force going through your hands all the way down to your feet. If you can't then there is a blockage somewhere: some tension has crept in or there is a misalignment of your skeleton that is preventing that direct connection from being made.

The next chapter will deal with how best to maintain this relaxing-down feeling when you're moving around.

Letting go

The ability to relax downwards is not as easy as it may first appear. One of the problems we face is that we do not want to let go of this tension. It is there for a reason; we have held on to it for years, it makes us feel safe and secure, how could we survive without it? For some people, these may sound like ridiculous questions but, believe me, this subconscious unwillingness to let go is the main reason why you're holding on to tension in the first place.

Letting go of the tension in our muscles means we are in danger of physical and emotional collapse.

Letting go of some of our deep-seated tensions means finally admitting to ourselves that stressful events have occurred in our lives. Often, particularly as young children, stressful situations are too much for us to cope with. We cannot process why they are happening and come to a satisfactory conclusion, so instead we lock them away behind a wall of tension. Releasing those deep-seated tensions can release the memories and energy. We can relive those bad times again and feel the raw emotions.

This sounds awful, but it can be very good for us. Now that we are adults we should have the intelligence, support systems and resourcefulness to be able to deal with those old issues. This could be emotionally very hard for a while, or we may sail straight through it with equanimity. Either way, we are finally free of those old traumas and, by going through this process, can release a lot of energy. I have come across many individuals who have released deep-seated tensions and have said afterwards that, for the first time in years, they were now able to see a positive future for themselves. The traumas of their past were no longer holding them back and they could stride forward in life with renewed confidence in their abilities.

Your tensions could be acting as an anchor, holding you back from what you want and deserve in life, or as walls locking away the darkest parts of yourself and hiding them from your conscious mind. Releasing that tension can knock down those walls and make that past come alive again. Know, though, that your subconscious mind is always protecting you. It protected you as a child by locking away things you weren't ready or able to deal with, and it will protect you now by only dissolving tensions and releasing traumas that you are able to cope with. It won't release everything at once, because that would overwhelm you and could cause irreparable damage. If traumas are deeply locked away, they may be released gradually so that you slowly become aware of the full extent of the trauma.

Dissolving tensions is like peeling an onion – layer after layer is gradually peeled away and sometimes the process involves a lot of tears.

Relaxing downwards exercise

This can be done anywhere; standing, sitting in a chair or on the floor or even lying down, though it is preferable to be vertical and aligned with gravity when you practise it.

From any of these positions, you apply the mental stabilisers. The five extremities can all be stabilised; the head from the chin, the hands or elbows and the feet or knees. Experiment so that you know where to apply the mental stabilisers for best effect.

1. If you are standing up, keep your knees slightly bent and imagine you are perched on a stool behind you. If you are sitting down, allow your lower back to rest more firmly on the chair, floor or whatever. Again this is a mental stabiliser and will help you to release tension in the lower body, particularly around the hips, and to direct the force of the upper body down through your legs and into the ground. Keep part of your focus on keeping the feet and lower legs weighted down.

2. Feel the weight in your elbows and knees; feel how that enables your shoulders and hips to let go.

3. Imagine you are standing under a waterfall and the water is rushing over your body, further dissolving all your tensions downwards.

4. Use your mind to scan your body for any tensions, areas of numbness, pain or uncomfortable feelings. If you find any, keep your mind there for a few moments until you feel a release as some of the tension dissolves.

5. Remember the expansion exercises from Chapter 3 and the expansion breath from Chapter 4. As you drop your tension downwards, allow yourself to expand at the same time as you breathe in, and further drop tensions downwards as you breathe out. This will help release your tension more effectively.

This powerful exercise can be done at any time; while waiting for a train, driving, doing the ironing or whatever. Your aim should be to practise it often enough that gradually you learn to relax downwards more all the time, and so actually hold on to less tension than before. You will be amazed at how much tension you are holding on to that you don't need. This exercise is even more effective when you feel stressed, as your tension levels will have shot up, but even when you're feeling relaxed you are still holding on to far more than you actually need. Your body will start to feel heavier and heavier, and for larger readers, please stop associating heaviness with fatness! From our perspective, heaviness is associated with a lack of tension, and is a great feeling to have.

Using the correct muscles to stabilise the skeleton and allowing your body to relax downwards makes it bottom-heavy – and this is a very good thing. Most people move from the head and shoulders, and their attention is focused on their head and their hands. They become top-heavy and this makes them unbalanced and more prone to any prevailing wind or opinion that comes their way. One of your main aims should be to drop the tension out of your body and into your legs. For this to happen, your legs need to – and will – become stronger; strong enough to properly support the weight of the upper body as they should.

So many people, and you may be one of them, feel that the world is a big, unfriendly place and they are a small insignificant person, too small to make a difference to the world. They feel that they are at the whim of every fashion, culture, peer pressure and media frenzy that comes their way. Imagine you are a cork in the ocean. You bob to and fro, totally at the mercy of every current. You have no power, no stability and no direction in life. You are like millions of people who follow the currents of life in the belief that they aren't big and strong enough to stand against the current, to be heard and taken seriously. Often the only way that people can feel safe and secure is to form groups, banding together with like-minded others – by religion, musical taste, sports team, political persuasion, etc.

'What has this to do with my posture?' I hear you ask. 'Absolutely everything!' I answer confidently.

People who are top-heavy are like corks in the ocean. Becoming bottom-heavy is like becoming a buoy, anchored to the seabed. No matter which way the currents go, you can resist them. You are connected to the earth, you are rooted to the whole planet, and this gives you strength enough to stand as an individual. You have already learned how to relax your body down into the ground, and it's well worth practising – in fact, it can change your whole life. You will feel much more rooted and stable and, by allowing all the parts of yourself to relax downwards through your strong legs and into the ground, you will be learning to work as one complete organism instead of a collection of parts.

Pressure-test your posture

I want you to try a little experiment now. For this you'll need another person.

1. Stand with your feet side by side, at least shoulder-width apart, with your partner to your side.

2. Ask your partner to push your shoulder gently from the side a few times to see how easily you move.

3. Now, without moving your feet, bend your knees slightly, ensure you are aligned with gravity, and drop your weight downwards into the ground.

4. As your partner pushes you, imagine a line from the point where they are pushing you down into your opposite foot – that is, left shoulder to right foot or vice versa – and don't allow that line to shorten. You should not allow your posture to collapse in any way but nor should you push back. Just allow the force to go through you and down into the ground. The more relaxed you are, the better this works. With just a little practice, someone can push you with all their strength and you will not move at all – and yet you will stay relaxed.

This is one of the first things I teach my kung fu students, to show them how a good structure will always be stronger than physical power.

You have just stayed relaxed and yet been unmoved by severe pressure just by changing the way you hold your body. True to the principle of the mind–body mirror, this same approach works for emotional and mental pressure. When faced with any kind of stressful situation, be aligned with gravity and drop as much weight downwards as you can. By doing so, you are consciously fighting your normal habitual reaction of tensing up. Of all the benefits of a good posture, this is perhaps the most important one.

When faced with any kind of stressful situation, be aligned with gravity and drop as much weight downwards as you can.

So, to recap: a good posture, the stress-free posture, is one which is aligned with gravity and any excess tension is allowed to drop downwards through the skeleton and into the ground. Allow your muscles to relax around your bones and trust that your skeleton is easily able to hold your weight upright. It should do: each bone may be incredibly light, but it is roughly eight times stronger than reinforced concrete. This is something you can and should practise any time, anywhere. Pull yourself upright, which in itself is a good way of toning the core muscles, and focus on different parts of your body, opening them and relaxing them downwards. Do not expect this to work for you in stressful situations if you haven't practised it regularly in nonstressful situations. Now we know how to stand; in the next chapter, we will use the same principles for our movements.

Janet realised that her posture was also adding to her panicked reaction to stress. One glance in the mirror confirmed that her posture was top-heavy. In fact, it looked as if she was being suspended by her shoulders. She tried the arm hang exercise and it felt amazing afterwards. Her shoulders seemed to drop by several inches. Unfortunately, the effect only lasted for a few minutes. She had no problem maintaining an upright stance, but relaxing it downwards seemed to be impossible. Clearly, she was stabilising herself using the wrong muscles. She tried the invisible stool and also imagining herself hanging from the top of the head instead of the shoulders. The effects of this were fast and dramatic. Her shoulders quickly dropped down. She tried to maintain the position for as long as she could while focusing on dropping her tension further. She recognises that she is battling against a lifetime's habits, but she is getting better every day and her reactions to stress are improving immeasurably.

Now that Peter had more energy due to his better breathing habits, he decided to pay more attention to his posture. He realised that he habitually held his head forward and dropped his chest on to his stomach. Lifting himself into a better position was a bit of a struggle as the tensions that held him there weren't going to give up easily. However, he could now breathe much more easily and realised he had to strengthen the muscles that held him in this position as well as release the tension up the front of his body. The more upright position made him feel much more self-confident and it also improved his bowel movements, which had been troubling him before. He had more energy and could move with more purpose now. It was time to get his life back.

A summary of Chapter 6

A good posture is one that is aligned with the forces acting on it and holds on to only as much tension as is necessary to maintain those forces in balance.

When the forces are allowed to flow through relaxed muscles and be diverted into the ground, then all kinds of physical and mental pressures/stresses can be withstood with relative equanimity.

To obtain the stress-proof posture four things need to occur: your legs need to become strong enough to support your full weight, your body should be upright - fully aligned with gravity, you should stabilise your joints appropriately and, most importantly, you should consciously relax *all* tensions downwards.

CHAPTER 7

Moving Without Tension

In this chapter

How can I stay relaxed when I'm moving around?

How can I make my movements less clumsy and unbalanced?

I often find myself leaning and looking at the ground when I'm walking. Is this bad for me and, if so, how can I stop it?

I find walking a chore rather than a pleasure. Is this because I'm not using my body properly?

It is one thing learning to stand or sit upright and drop tension out of your body when you are standing or sitting still. It is quite another thing to maintain a perfectly aligned position and maintain the feeling of relaxing downwards when you are moving around.

What happens is that you spend some time sitting or standing and focusing on dropping the tensions out of your posture but, as soon as you start to move, your old, habitual ways of moving take over. Instinctively you raise your shoulders to lift your arms, develop tension in your hips and buttocks to stabilise your legs and so on. One of the most important aspects of tai chi chuan (when it is taught properly) is that it teaches you to learn to move your body without holding on to unnecessary tension. It takes some time to learn, or rather to unlearn, the poor habits of a lifetime. This chapter is all about making you aware of what's happening in your body when you move. It gives you plenty of practical advice to help you make your body more efficient and tension-free.

There is no other art in the world like tai chi chuan. It alone teaches perfect efficiency of movement. There is much more to the art than that, but that is our focus here. Unfortunately, the movements may be highly efficient, but the way it is taught seldom is. It is a traditional Chinese art and the word 'traditional' in China usually means Confucian. The Confucian way of teaching demands respect from student to master, obedience to all instructions and no questions asked.

It is almost universal in classes that are taught the Confucian way that the master will tell the students what to do and show them the movements required but will rarely, if ever, explain the principles behind the movements. It is expected that the students should be able to work out the principles for themselves. If they cannot, then they aren't worthy of them or yet at a level to understand them. This is the way I was taught, and it has taken me over twenty years to work out the principles behind the marvellous skills I was taught and to be able to bring the same effortless power to any movement. Without the knowledge of these principles, I would be restricted to teaching the techniques I was taught by rote, hoping that I was remembering them correctly. Now that I understand the principles, I know for sure that I am doing the skills correctly and I am able to modify any technique to changing circumstances, secure in the knowledge that, as long as it follows the correct principles, it will work effectively. It is these principles that I have had to work out for myself over many years of trial and error that I present to you in this book.

Virtually all tai chi forms begin with a simple movement – raising and lowering the arms. Yet within this simple movement lies a wealth of detail and instruction. This isn't a tai chi book, but it is largely about efficient posture, movement and breath. The lesson we can learn here from tai chi is clear. When learning to move with natural, efficient grace, it is best to start with simple movements or tasks that require little or no conscious input; in other words, tasks or movements that you have done before so often that they have become a habit. When you are doing a habitual action, your conscious mind doesn't need to keep its mind on the job and so it often leaves the body and thinks about something else. This is efficient; you can be emptying the washing machine and planning tomorrow's work at the same time. Unfortunately, your mind, like everyone else's, demands to be kept active, so if the task at hand is a repetitive one your mind will find some way of busying itself, often with negative thought patterns.

One way to break negative thought patterns is to pay far more conscious attention to what you are doing and how you are doing it.

What I want you to do now is find a simple task and make it conscious; in other words, really focus on it. Put your mind in your body and become aware of your balance, alignments, and where you are holding on to tension. Apply the principles of relaxing downwards, stabilising with various different parts of your body in different positions; relax your elbows and knees down to keep tension out of the hips and shoulders. In doing so, you will be going against the habitual way you have done this task in the past. You will be learning new and healthier ways of achieving the same purpose as well as new and healthier ways of using your own body. When you don't need to think about anything else, then you can focus fully on what you are doing and how you are doing it. This is a powerful practice of self-awareness; in fact, it is meditation in motion. At first it may sound boring – your ego rebels against it – but try it and you will soon discover just how pleasurable it can be. One of the main goals of Daoism (and this series of books) is to allow your mind and body to become one, to do away with the duality of the Western world that seeks to separate mind and matter.

The 'walk of awareness'

Have you ever watched the way other people walk? We may all be built to the same basic blueprints, but the amount of variety in the way we propel ourselves forward is amazing. Each of the people you see clearly believe that the way they are walking is the most effective for them at that time. Why is there such a variety in their walks? There are many answers to this: habit, personality, the needs of the moment and internal tensions.

As tension gradually builds in the body, it generates enormous forces in the musculoskeletal system, which bends it out of shape and prevents muscles from moving joints freely along the path they are designed to take. Any imbalances that throw your body out of perfect alignment will cause extra tension in other muscles. That tension needs to be there to prevent you from toppling over. Tension spreads and a leg muscle that may pull the knee out of alignment will then affect the foot and the hip, which will affect your spine, which may affect your shoulders and neck... Naturally, this will affect the way you walk as well as sit, stand and do any other movements. Note that this is a gradual change and one you may not even notice. Just as children grow gradually taller without you noticing, so your walk can change gradually and becomes less free and easy.

The majority of people move their body habitually from their shoulders or, worse still, the head, most of the time. As these areas are at the top of the body, it means the top leads and the bottom follows. You can see this done in an exaggerated way in many cartoons. When you think about it, the problems with this become obvious. This head-leading form of motion puts extra weight in front of your body so that you can swing your back leg forward and the forward-thrust head then drops your body weight onto your front leg. This works —after a fashion – but it is not how we are designed to walk.

The majority of people move their body habitually from their shoulders or, worse still, the head, most of the time.

This method of falling forward onto your front leg is far from being a healthy action. It means you are never really aligned properly with gravity, and so the muscles of the back and neck can never let go of their tension otherwise you'd stumble forwards. This means that every step you take requires more energy than it should and so you get tired more quickly than you need to.

Your body is designed to be held upright when walking. There are muscles in the front and back of the hips and legs that are specifically designed for our two-legged mode of locomotion. The commonly seen head-leading, body falling onto the front foot way of walking leads to weakness in these muscles as well as tightness up the front of the body. I'm afraid it means you are going to have to relearn how to walk – but don't worry, it's painless. As always, I'll give you the principles you need to know, and I have tried to limit the things you need to think about to the most essential.

Your body is designed to be held upright when walking.

Find your centre

Roughly two to three inches below your navel is your centre of gravity. Were you to lie across a metal bar and use your back, bottom and leg muscles to keep you parallel to the ground, that is the only point at which you could be balanced. It is also an important point in many Eastern philosophies and traditions, where it is often seen as a *chakra*, a source of energy or an area where energy is stored. Being your body's centre of balance as well as being the main pivot point of the body, it is also a crucial area to focus on regarding posture and movement. As if all that wasn't enough, it is here, at the centre of the body, where you digest and process your food (the Chinese believe that emotions are also processed in this area).

Whether you're sitting, standing, walking or running, your body is constantly trying to balance the forces that are at work upon it. There is the ever-present down-force of gravity keeping you attached to the planet. Added to this are the muscular forces at work within you as you push down on alternate legs to swing your body forward for walking or hold your arms in front of you to iron shirts, and so on. On top of these forces are any external forces that may be acting upon you, such as a heavy wind, a bag of shopping or an unstable bicycle. To balance these forces efficiently means all parts of your body should become involved in each movement, as they will all certainly be affected.

When you are trying to move something heavy like a wardrobe you would quickly realise the futility of trying to move it from the top – assuming you could even reach it, that is! It is far more efficient to move it from the centre or even further down depending on how much friction there is with the carpet. Your body is the same. Trying to move it from the head is truly inefficient. Not only will it force the rest of your structure to bend forward, but it is at the furthest point from your legs. Moving it from the legs would be better, but could mean you end up leaning backwards as your head struggles to keep up.

The only sensible answer is to do what martial artists have been doing for many centuries – to move from the centre of the body. In this way, both lower and upper halves of the body are being moved together and so it is easier to remain upright. Moving from your centre may feel slightly strange at first, but you will quickly get used to it when you realise it has many benefits: it enables you to get where you're going with less expenditure of energy; you will spend less time leaning forward and looking down, so you will become more aware of your environment; and you will look and feel far more confident and appear less like a victim. Naturally, you are also far less likely to hold on to the tensions and stresses of your day if you are standing and walking upright and relaxed.

By learning to use your body properly, you can look forward
to an active old age, less hampered by postural problems.

Be pulled along

I'll assume that now you have some familiarity with the postural points I mentioned above – namely, being upright and aligned with gravity and relaxing your tensions downwards. All you need do is maintain these points when moving, and the easiest way to do that is to move from your centre. I have discovered another principle that will make it even easier for you to move smoothly and powerfully, when needed, from your centre.

When you are walking along, imagine that you are being pulled forward gently from the waist. This passive feeling of being pulled along, or pushed from behind if you prefer, is wonderfully easy and powerful. It feels like you are no longer applying the force yourself but just moving your legs enough to keep up with the gentle force that's moving you. Your upper body can remain upright and relaxed and your arms can swing freely, giving in to the force of gravity that's gently pulling them downwards. Your leg muscles are now working as they should, with the hip flexors pulling the unweighted leg forward and the big muscles of the calf, back of the leg and buttocks effortlessly driving your body forward. Don't forget to keep the weight in your elbows and knees and to look straight ahead to prevent your head from dropping forward.

Now imagine you're walking along, alert and relaxed, when you come to an uphill section. In the old days (before you read this book) you would lean forward further and increase the tension in the upper body in a vague attempt to pull yourself up the hill. No more. Now feel your centre being pulled up the hill, keep the upper body relaxed and use your legs efficiently to get you up there. Remember that the stronger your legs become, the less tension you will need in your upper body. I have tried this many times when doing hill walks. Just focus on a point some way ahead of you and imagine that you are being pulled towards this point from your waist. This same principle applies to walking upstairs as well. Try to stay aligned and be pulled forwards from your centre and legs. You should no longer need handrails to balance or to pull you up the stairs, unless your posture is still unbalanced. If that's the case, keep working on the principles in this book and you too may be able to walk with balanced confidence up and down stairs with ease.

Talking about downstairs and down hills, you can apply the same principles. However, this time imagine a rope around your waist that's extending up the hill or stairs behind you and that you are gradually being lowered down. This will enable you to remain balanced, aligned and stable while you negotiate the downward slope. Most people find going downhill or downstairs more challenging than going up. Certainly children take a lot longer to master going downstairs than going up. Going down a slope requires you to use your leg muscles as brakes to absorb the increased force of gravity.

The stronger your legs become, the less tension you will need in your upper body.

Walk like a cat

One of the reasons cats make such popular pets is that we all admire the power and grace of their movements. Cats are masters of everything I teach in this book. They can be completely relaxed, holding on to no unneeded tension, then suddenly become a blur of power and movement. Cats understand how to use their bodies in the most efficient way. One of the things they instinctively understand is that their muscles aren't just to move their frame but also serve to cushion the impact of their movements. The muscles in their upper and lower legs serve as shock absorbers and are connected to their spine, which acts as a flexible bridge to further cushion the shock of landing from on high. You will rarely, if ever, see a cat completely straighten its legs. It does so only when leaping for maximum height, then it

114

instantly bends them again to precisely gauge its landing and to cushion the impact.

Unlike cats, many humans straighten their knees regularly when standing and with every step they take. A straightened knee cannot absorb force, so the force travels straight up to the hips. A lot of time spent standing with straight knees can damage the knee joints and put excess strain on the hip joints. Learn to move with your knees slightly soft at all times. Your legs may ache a little at first, as they are now being used properly to cushion your walking or running impact, but they will soon strengthen up. Your walk will be smoother and stronger and you should feel more connected and more confident. Keeping a slightly bent knee also lowers your centre of gravity so makes you more stable. The muscles that surround and support the knee joint will strengthen, which will make future knee injuries less likely.

One other thing you may notice about a cat is its elongated feet. That joint at the back that many people mistake for a knee joint is in fact its ankle. It does have a heel bone but it doesn't use it for walking in the way we do. Its calf muscles and ankle joint give it a further dimension of both power and impact control. Again this is something we can emulate.

Try not to spend too much time standing or walking on your heels. When walking, either put the foot flat on the floor or the heel down first but either way aim to get your weight in front of the heel as soon as possible. By doing so you now have the power and springiness of the ankle and calf muscles to power and support your next move. Again, it's a question of learning to use the body more efficiently so that you have more power where you really need it and hold on to less tension where you don't. When standing, bring your weight forward slightly so that your weight comes slightly in front of your heels. Use the triangle formed by the ball of the big toe, the pad of the big toe and the ball of the little toe to stand. If your weight goes backwards, you can rock back onto your heels. If you're already on your heels and your weight goes backwards you must either step back or fall over! If, however, you are standing properly and your weight goes backwards then your heels act as a backstop to prevent you falling on your behind.

The five points of awareness

One of the most useful practices you can apply when moving is to focus your attention on your five peripheral points: your two hands, your two feet and your head. With even a small amount of practice you will start to feel how these five points relate to each other in your movements. This will dramatically improve your balance and grace and enable you to know where in your body to apply power to achieve your movement goal. For example, if you'd stepped forward with your right foot and were about to pick up a heavy bag of groceries with your right hand instead of just straightening your back and lifting with your arms, you should also apply downward force through your right leg. This will balance the upward movement of the upper body and make it far stronger. It will spread the load, thus taking a lot of strain off your back muscles. This ability to spread a load among as much of the body's musculature as possible has been developed and practised in China in kung fu schools for centuries. It enables the practitioner to develop or withstand huge forces through holding the body correctly and using leverage and unified muscle power. The practice of this comes largely through understanding the five points of awareness.

Use your legs as much as possible. They will take much of the strain that before was taken by your back, shoulders or neck muscles.

The walk of awareness

1. Maintain the principles of posture that you have learned – stay upright and relax downwards.

2. Feel yourself being pulled forward from the centre of your body.

3. Keep your knees slightly bent and your weight in front of your heels as much as possible.

4. Try to maintain awareness of how you are walking, particularly the five points of awareness and also the external environment through which you are walking.

If you are able to maintain the points above then any walk, from a trip to the kitchen to a mountain hike, will become more of a pleasure, will help you to turn these healthy principles into habits, and will lengthen the useful life of your body.

Run like a tiger

For those of you who like to run, please bear in mind the principles above and follow the points below:

Keep the knees soft at all times to protect the joints.

Don't lean forwards or backwards when running – stay upright to allow your upper body to relax downwards.

Feel yourself being drawn forward from your centre. This will keep your upper body aligned and minimise the energy needed to maintain the run.

Keep the weight in your elbows to keep your shoulders down and aligned with your body.

Run like a tiger by allowing as much of your weight as possible to go down through your legs and into the ground. This will increase your contact with the ground and so make your forward movement more powerful and effortless.

Remember to breathe through your nose to increase your stamina.

Breath and posture together

Now that you know the basics of a good posture – alignment, internal stability and relaxing downwards – you can now add your breathing skills to further stress-proof your body.

The expansion breath is what you need to practise. This should gradually become your default mode of breathing. The expansion breath ties in very closely with the three posture points mentioned in this and the previous chapter.

First, only when you are upright and aligned with gravity can your breathing spaces be fully opened. Any time you are out of alignment it will cause compression or collapse somewhere in your posture. This will prevent you from being able to breathe fully. One of the worst things you can do, and something that most people spend a lot of time doing, is to allow your chest to collapse downwards onto your stomach. This compresses all your digestive organs and prevents you from being able to use your diaphragm to breathe properly. It's a double whammy effect – you have far less oxygen and energy coming in and you are preventing most of your essential organs from working properly. I am positive this is one of the factors leading to obesity, as food cannot be digested efficiently in this position and so is laid down as fat deposits. Also, as most people know, your body can only burn fat in the presence of oxygen, so if your breathing is poor little oxygen is getting in and so little of your fat can be burned. Learn to take slower, fuller breaths with a good posture and your system can operate as it should, so virtually everything you do will become aerobic, hence fat-burning, exercise.

A good posture is one that allows a full breath to be taken.

Second, your expansion breath will gradually open up the blockages inside you and fill you with your breathing, and this will support your internal structure and stability. Strange as it may sound, it does work very well. As you become more aware of what's going on inside you, your breath will help you to feel which parts of you are closed off with tension, preventing you from unifying your body from within. In fact, it is most people's inability to use their diaphragm to breathe properly that creates excess tension in the upper body and separates it from the hips and legs. Learning to open up your centre and breathe into it will connect the upper and lower halves of your body and enable you to relax the tensions of the upper body down through your legs into the floor. That is why I taught you to breathe before I taught you to stand. If your centre is closed and you habitually breathe into your chest, it is virtually impossible for you to relax downwards through your posture and release your tensions.

Posture and breathing go together. It isn't possible to breathe well with a poor posture. It also isn't possible to maintain and support a good posture with faulty breathing habits.

Third, your exhalations will enable you to breathe out your tensions and relax them downwards more fully. As we saw in Chapter 4, each exhalation releases tension and you can even focus your mind on a particular area and imagine exhaling out tensions from that point.

To recap on the expansion breath, as you inhale you focus on opening up the inside of you, allowing more and more parts of yourself to open up to your breath. As you exhale, you relax your tensions downwards while maintaining that expanded and open feeling.

Finally, here is the companion to the dragon's back exercise you learned in the last chapter. This exercise is called the snake's back and it mobilises the spine laterally and helps to balance the muscles on either side of the spine, all the way up into the neck.

The snake's back exercise

1. Stand aligned with your feet about hip-width apart, feet facing forward and knees slightly bent.

2. Raise your arms to the sides around or just below shoulder height.

3. Tilt your hips from side to side, pushing down through one foot and then the other. As you continue the movement, aim to gradually release the tension in the spine, feel the area opening up and allowing movement through. Gradually you will feel a wave of movement going laterally up the spine like the movement of a snake.

4. Continue the movement for twenty to thirty seconds and gradually increase the time.

To start with, the movement may feel a bit jerky but, with practice, the muscles surrounding the spine open up and the whole body moves in a sinuously wavy pattern that goes from the hips all the way up to the head and down into the feet. The movement also travels out in a wave through the alternate arms moving the shoulder, elbow, wrist and fingers. When you can achieve this, you have the snake's back.

Peter realised that he habitually walked leading with his head, looking down at the pavement in front of him. His mind was elsewhere and the constant tension down the back of his body that prevented him from falling forwards was largely responsible for him feeling so tired. So he practised staying upright and moving from his centre. Immediately he felt lighter and more connected to his environment. He had more of a natural spring in his step and he realised he could walk much further without tiring himself out.

Janet still struggled with relaxing her tensions downwards. However, she learned that maintaining a feeling of weight in her knees and elbows helped her to drop the tension out of her hips and shoulders as she walked. She learned to keep her knees soft and to feel the ground beneath her feet. She imagined herself to be a cat, moving with relaxed power. It was wonderful; she felt so much more powerful and better able to cope with the pressures of her day.

A summary of Chapter 7

Maintaining the principles that prevent the build-up of tension is more difficult when moving than when standing or sitting still.

Try to generate all movements from the centre of the body. Relax your weight into the ground. This improves your connection with the earth, and the increased force travels up your legs into your centre. Let it move your centre and let your arms be moved by your centre. Don't use your arms alone to begin any movement or to apply force. Let the force come from the legs, be directed through the waist and expressed through the hands.

Develop the walk of awareness and use it every day. It will carry you effortlessly through your life.

When doing any movement, particularly one that requires you to apply any kind of force, be aware of the five peripheral points of the body. This will help you spread the load throughout your body.

Use your expansion breath combined with your posture to help you to maintain good alignments, release more tension and learn to use your whole body in all your actions.

CHAPTER 8

Your Flexible Body

In this chapter

Why is flexibility seen as so important in the Eastern cultures?

I have tried doing stretching exercises before but never really seem to get any more flexible. What am I doing wrong?

As I get older I seem to get stiffer and stiffer. Can stretching really help me to regain my mobility and feel younger?

At the beginning of the introduction I said that the more tense you are, the older you feel. Tension robs you of movement, pits muscle against muscles and drains you of energy. Regaining flexibility is like regaining your youth. Suddenly things become easier again, you have more energy, you aren't fighting yourself with every movement and so your body will last longer.

Flexibility is one of the cornerstones of gaining a stress-proof body. In this chapter we look at why flexibility is so important and how best to achieve it. We see that we can use the same principles we learned in Chapter 6 on posture. You will see that flexibility isn't just about releasing tension in certain areas, but is also about gaining core strength that will enable you to stand and move with less effort and more power.

Imagine if you could have a bath in WD40. It would seep into all your joints, restoring them to their full range of motion, lubricating every part until it was as new and dissolving away all the tension. What would that feel like? Every movement would now be so easy. With no tension to prevent full movement, you would feel unbelievably free. Every movement your body makes would be a pleasure instead of a chore. With no tension to slow you down or fight against, everything would be effortless. You would breeze through the day and enjoy every part of it with an amazing feeling of freedom and lightness.

This is what flexibility training can do for you. It opens up your joints, loosens the tension and restores a fuller range of movement throughout your body. In doing so, it also gives you more energy as less of your energy is being spent in fighting your tensions.

These huge benefits alone should be more than enough motivation to get you to stretch daily – but it doesn't stop there:

Stretching helps prevent injuries and pain as your body isn't fighting itself with every move it makes. Most injuries are caused either by excessive tension in muscles or joints being moved beyond their normal range of movement. Flexibility training can help with both of these. Stretching helps prevent post-exercise pain (DOMS – Delayed Onset Muscle Soreness) and stiffness, and it improves your blood circulation which in turn helps with blood pressure and takes some of the strain off your heart – which is great news for those with cold hands and feet in the winter. Finally, stretching improves your posture by regaining a fuller range of movement in each joint and so allowing your posture to regain its balance, free of conflicting pulls and forces.

The more flexible you are, the more you are able to relax.
The more you are able to relax, then the easier flexibility is
to attain. It is a virtuous circle.

This point is a very important one. It is at those times when you are feeling very tense and unable to relax that doing stretching exercises will do you the most good. You may well feel too tired to stretch, but it is then that opening your joints and stretching your muscles is exactly what you need. If you had 10 minutes spare, you could lie down for those 10 minutes then get up feeling only slightly less tense or you could do five minutes of stretches and lie down for the other five minutes. The second option would leave you feeling far more refreshed and invigorated. For those of you who find it difficult to sleep at night, why not try doing some stretches just before you get into bed? Remember, *the more flexible you are, the more you are able to relax.* I do this most nights and find it helps me to drop off to sleep more quickly and to sleep more soundly. Maybe it will work for you too.

As we saw in Chapter 5, flexibility is something that we gradually lose from the moment we are born. I well remember playing with my daughter when she was a baby, holding one leg on the floor and lifting the other leg all the way up to tickle her on the nose. She giggled with delight, as there was no tension in her legs or back to cause her any discomfort. Now, however, she is five years old and I was dismayed the other day to see that she is now unable to touch her toes while keeping her knees straight. This goes to show how quickly suppleness is lost – even in someone who is very active and full of energy. I can easily touch my toes and go way beyond that, so there is hope for us all when a man in his late forties can be more flexible than a five-year-old girl. The reason I am more flexible than her is simply that I do specific flexibility training. It can take a while to become supple but the small amount of time and effort you need to put in are well worth it.

Even a small gain in flexibility can pay great dividends to your posture and the way you feel about yourself.

Flexibility is joint-specific. You can be very supple in some joints while having very little movement in others. You will also find that your range of movement (ROM) in each joint varies from hour to hour. Hence you can get a good idea of how tense you are and where you habitually hold on to tension by doing a range of stretching exercises.

It is interesting how in the West we view stamina as the most important aspect of fitness whereas in the East flexibility is seen as more essential. We consider stamina to be important because it is seen as helping us to control our weight and protect our hearts, which of course is true. So why is flexibility seen as more important in the Eastern cultures? Chiefly because it is seen as an effective path to rid the body of tensions and as you have learned it is your tensions that are causing most of the pain and misery prompts our trips to the Doctors.

Can flexibility help with heart disease and weight control too? I believe the answer is a big yes to both. Briefly, by releasing the tension and opening up your joints there is less muscular tension to restrict blood flow which takes a significant load off the heart. There has been little scientific research done into this so far but all that has been done has shown promising results. As for weight loss the celebrity world is full of singers, models and actors who find that regular yoga or other stretching routines keeps them in touch with their body and maintains the good posture that is necessary to digest their food properly. By doing so they are able to maintain their body at a healthy weight more easily. It's certainly worth a try and if nothing else you will definitely release a lot of the tension that's holding you back, causing you pain and increasing your stress.

Hard and soft tension

Anybody who is used to stretching exercises will be familiar with what I term 'soft' tension. This is the feeling you get when you wake up in the morning and try to touch your toes and can get barely past your knees. You are aware that this isn't the permanent limit of your flexibility, and with a few warming-up movements and some gentle stretching you can regain and reach your true limit, however far down that may be. Your true flexibility of that joint is limited by 'hard' tension. The hard tension marks the extreme limits of your movements, but it can and will be gradually softened by regular stretching.

Your aim is to turn hard tension into soft tension into no tension.

It is important to understand the concept of soft tension as it marks a boundary between your current range of movement and your true range of movement. This means that when you do a stretching exercise and meet resistance it is likely that this is temporary, soft resistance and with a little effort – and using an efficient technique – you can go through this to find the barriers of your hard tension. Many people get discouraged when stretching as they discover how small their range of movement is in different joints. However, it may well be that the resistance they come to is just soft tension which, with just a little persistence, can be pushed back.

As you move a joint to towards the end of its range of movement, resistance starts to build up. If you move quickly into any extended position, then the muscles will contract to prevent the joint from being injured. This is soft tension, and this can quickly harden if the body feels the joint is at serious risk of injury. Your aim is to prevent the tension from hardening and limiting your range of movement. However, follow the guidelines below and your stretches will be both safe and effective.

The role of core strength

Your aim is to develop a balanced body, one that has flexibility and mobility in the muscles that move joints and core strength in the muscles that support your frame.

Essentially, there are two types of stretches: passive stretches that use gravity, leverage or a partner to apply the force, and active stretches that use your own muscles to apply the force.

Generally speaking, stretches that you do standing up will use gravity to apply the force, so they will be passive stretches. A good example is touching your toes. You bend forward at the waist and gravity pulls your head and trunk downward, thus applying force to the lower back and hamstrings to stretch them. We'll go into this in more detail later.

Stretches that you perform from a seated or lying position tend to use your own muscles for power. This is where the development of core strength comes in. If we take the toe-touching exercise again, this is easier done standing up as gravity pulls you down. If you try to sit down with your legs extended in front of you then push yourself forward, you would probably lack the core strength to overcome the tension in the back and hamstrings. You may even lack the strength to pull your spine upright instead of being pushed back from the lower spine. With regular practice, core strength increases and the tension it is fighting against decreases and you can push yourself further into the stretch.

Flexibility training gives you extra strength in the deep muscles that stabilise and move the body. This in turn gives you a much greater range of movement.

Your new-found mobility and flexibility will transfer to any sport or activity you engage in.

How to stretch

There are many ways to stretch, and many books on the subject. Unfortunately, as with so many other areas of human health and development, there are no definitive answers and much of the research that has been carried out has contradictory findings. One example of this is the assertion that you should isolate the specific muscle you want to stretch as much as possible. By doing so, you don't have to work against the resistance from other muscles involved in the same movement. There are two problems with this that I can see. First, all our physical movements are carried out by a range of muscles and not by specific isolated muscles. Hence our stretching should be to increase the range of a movement as it would be used. Attempting to stretch only very specific muscles by holding them in unnecessarily fixed positions could throw the body out of balance. Trust in the innate intelligence of your body and allow it to open up the joints and release the tension where it feels best. The second and more pragmatic reason is that to effectively stretch each muscle in isolation is likely to take a good two or more hours. Very few people have this luxury of time on a regular basis.

I will give some guidelines that will enable you to develop your own stretching routine. Each of us is built differently, and nobody knows your body better than you do. Within a very short time, you will know it a lot better and will have a good idea of which joints are stiff and which are fairly mobile. You will know where the limits of your hard tension are and which movements are often restricted by soft tension. Furthermore, you will get to know where in your body you tend to hold on to tension during the day and so can work out quick maintenance stretches to release that tension and keep you fresh throughout the day. Generally, your aim should be to reduce the tension surrounding the stiffest joints, although this may be less satisfactory and fun than moving your more mobile joints.

The golden rules of stretching

Relax the area you're stretching. Your aim is to release – not increase – tension. You cannot stretch a tight muscle.

Move slowly and smoothly into each position. When a joint is moved quickly towards the end of its range of movement, the muscles surrounding it automatically tighten up to prevent injury. As you are aiming to relax the muscles and release that tension, this would clearly be counterproductive. So move slowly and smoothly into each position so as not to trigger soft tension that would then need to be released before you can work on the harder tension.

Balance your stretches. This means that you should stretch both sides of the body equally and both sides of a joint. For example, you shouldn't stretch just the left hamstrings without also stretching the ones on the right leg. You should also aim to stretch both sets of quadriceps at the same time (these oppose the hamstrings) and also the other main muscles which assist in part of their range of movement, in this case the calf muscles and the gluteal muscles in the buttocks.

If you are unfamiliar with muscle names and actions, it's a good idea to learn the main ones. After all, they are your muscles, they are tight and are affecting your health and wellbeing. There aren't that many to learn and it's another way to get to know yourself better. When you are stretching, you will soon learn which movements are difficult for you, so learn which muscles are involved in those movements, their location and where their two, or more, ends connect.

Types of stretching

Let's quickly examine the main types of stretching.

Ballistic stretching. This is how stretching used to be done. It involves bouncing in and out of a stretched position. Now it is considered to be relatively ineffective and potentially dangerous as the muscles are given no time to relax within the stretch. It is no longer recommended for general training but is specific to certain sports. Even then, it should be done only when thoroughly warmed up and other stretches have been done.

Dynamic stretching. This involves slow, controlled movements towards the end of your range of movement and then repeating or switching sides. With each repetition you are gradually aiming to increase your range of movement. You move towards the soft tension then, with each repetition, push gently through it until you reach the hard tension. This is one of the most beneficial types of stretching and will gradually show you your real limits. It is the type of stretching that I do the most and is wonderful for releasing soft tension during the day and keeping you moving freely. This is the most common and beneficial form of Maintenance Stretching (see below).

Static stretching. Perhaps the most common type of stretching. The joint is moved to the end of its range of movement and held there. Fifteen seconds is good for a beginner, gradually increasing up to forty to sixty seconds. Within ten to fifteen seconds you should feel a slight release in the joint as some of the soft tension is released. This will enable you to relax further into the stretch.

There are two types of static stretching – active, where you use your own muscles to hold a joint in a stretched position and passive, where you use another force, usually gravity, to hold it in position.

PNF stretching. If you want to impress people, you can tell them that PNF stands for proprioceptive neuromuscular facilitation. This type of stretching is generally held to be one of the most effective types of stretching, but it is a more advanced technique. It is an intense stretch, so it is vital that the muscles are *thoroughly* warmed up for at least five minutes before this is attempted. No more than two to three sets per session should be attempted for each muscle group.

What you do is warm up the area first then hold a static stretch for around ten seconds. Then you contract the muscle, against resistance, for about five seconds, release the contraction then increase the stretch and hold it for thirty seconds. I have developed a stretching method which gives excellent results, but without being as risky as PNF stretching, and I will discuss this next.

The stretch reflex

The stretch reflex is one of your natural defences against being injured.

Basically, if you try to stretch a joint towards the limit of its range of movement too quickly then the muscle spindles send an alarm message to the brain warning of impending danger, i.e. that the muscle or joint may be torn or otherwise damaged. To prevent this, a message is sent to the muscle to contract to prevent damage to the joint.

In practical terms, this means that if you try to stretch too hard or too quickly the muscle you're trying to stretch will contract, which is the opposite of what you're trying to achieve. In order to stretch it, you need it to trust that you're not going to damage it. There are two methods I find useful to prevent the stretch reflex kicking in and ruining your stretch.

The first is to stabilise the joint just when you hit the soft tension, i.e. as soon as you start to feel any tightening. When I say 'stabilise', I mean physically prevent it from going any further. If I was doing a forward bend to touch my toes, I would rest my hands on my knees or upper legs to prevent any further downward movement. However, I would continue to gently push my spine forwards and downwards as if continuing the movement. The muscles would realise that this movement was safe and no damage could occur and so would happily release more tension. After a few seconds, I could release that stabilising hold and easily go down further, again going nowhere near the hard tension, and stabilise it again for a few seconds, maintaining the gentle pressure. Quite quickly I'd reach the hard tension and could stabilise it again to see if I could make any further gains. When you have reached as far as you can, you should hold for a good thirty seconds to allow the tendons and muscles to acclimatise to the new length and so not generate so much tension next time around.

In this way you can also fine-tune your stretches to emphasise certain muscles or parts of muscles to stretch. The more you can turn your hard tension into softer tension, the more flexibility you will have to change the stretches that you do in subtle ways. You will find that keeping certain muscles slightly tense while stretching will change which parts of other muscles get stretched. This probably sounds more complicated than it is. There are many books on this subject, particularly on yoga although, as always, finding a good class is the best way to learn.

The second method is what I call Passive Small Movement (PSM) stretching. This is a form of dynamic stretches that keep the joints open and mobile throughout the stretch. Sometimes in static stretches you can unwittingly lock certain joints into position and this will limit how far you are able to go into the stretch. PSM stretching prevents this by keeping all the joints mobile. It also uses your mind to create the motive force.

The mind–body connection is a remarkable thing and is not yet completely understood by science. In PSM stretching we use our mind to soften the areas being stretched and to apply the stretching force in the exercises.

When doing any stretch, use your mind to apply a *gentle*, imaginary force to any part of the body. A simple example is the forward bend where you're sitting down with your feet extended in front of you. To do a forward bend, you could push yourself forward in the hope of grabbing your feet and being able to pull yourself forward with your hands. I find it more powerful to imagine that I'm being pulled forward instead of pushing myself forward. Pushing creates excess tension in areas that I don't want to be tense. Being pulled, on the other hand, is a passive process which my body is allowing to happen. I simply extend my arms forward and imagine them being pulled forward towards my feet. Clearly I am still doing the movement myself, but the way I'm doing it has changed. Feeling yourself being pulled into a stretch is also more pleasurable and easier than pushing yourself into it. This is how you do it:

Passive Small Movement stretching method

1. Imagine yourself being gently pulled into a stretched position and stop just as you feel the resistance but maintain that gentle. imaginary force pulling you further.

2. Make small movements with any or all of the relevant joints while maintaining that stretched position. These small movements should help your muscles and joints align with the direction of the force that you are visualising.

3. After a few moments you should find you can be pulled by the visualised force further into the stretch. Again make the small movements, particularly around the hips and torso to loosen up the tension and enable more movement into the stretch.

4. When you have reached your true limit of hard tension, with no pain, then hold for at least 15 seconds. While you are holding it,

focus on the areas that feel and visualise them expanding and opening up. The expansion breath is great for this.

5. Always remember to stretch both sides of your body and the muscles on both sides of a joint.

When you first start stretching most, if not all, of your tension will be fairly hard. Moving slowly to and then gently through that tension and doing so regularly will soften that hard tension and enable you to go a little further. As I said earlier, don't expect huge gains overnight – although you may find that the tension you thought was limiting isn't as hard as you thought and will soften up quite quickly, enabling reasonable gains to be made swiftly. This will encourage you to carry on.

Daily practice is the only assured way to regain the flexibility that is your right and it is virtually the only path to a happy and healthy body.

Like many people, I do some stretching exercises first thing in the morning. After a night's sleep with little body movement the tension creeps up and my body feels tight and tense. So I spend about ten minutes gently stretching out – sideways stretches, forwards, backwards and stretching the front of my hips, inner legs and fronts of my legs. I use dynamic stretches followed by the PSM method of stretching and all I am doing here is pushing back the boundaries of my temporary tension until I have regained what I consider to be my natural limits. Then my body feels light and free and I'm not fighting my body with every move I make. If I have time, then I will spend longer on certain stretches and work on softening the areas of hard tension that are limiting me.

In short, stretching is one of the main ways in which you can combat the encroaching tides of tension that can engulf and freeze your body and mind.

Maintenance Stretches

It's been a hard morning sat at your desk and your body is starting to feel like it's solidified with tension. You don't have time for proper stretching exercises so what can you do? Simple. Just go through some dynamic movements slowly increasing your range of movement in a few key areas and this will release all that nasty soft tension that's locking up your body and paralysing your mind.

The two minute tension buster.

1. Start with side bends. It's amazing how much tension seems to be stored up the sides of the body. Just raise your left arm, drop your shoulder blade down and lean to the right until you feel a little tightening then lower the arm, raise the other one and lean the other way until that tightens, then repeat. Do this just a few times and each time you will be able to lean over further. Try to keep your shoulder blades down throughout the movement.

2. Now forward and backward bends. Slowly and smoothly, raise your arms above your head, look upwards then bend forward at the waist and as you go down bring your arms up behind your back and look dowarwards. Now lower your hands to the floor and straighten up again raising your hands back up above your head and look up again. Repeat a few times to loosen the tension and increase your range of movement. As always never force anything.

3. Finally do some leg swings. Swing one leg at a time back and forward to loosen the hips. You may need to hold onto something for stability.

That's it. In two minutes or less you have released a lot of your soft tension and should be ready to get back to your desk and face your in tray again. You're amazed at how much better you feel.

Stretch your front

As we noticed in Chapter 2, tension builds up on both sides of a joint. When one side becomes so tight that the muscles on the other side of the joint aren't strong enough to balance it, the joint is forced to move, to bend; this often causes a C shape somewhere in the posture.

The causes for the C shape are many and varied (see Chapter 2) but it is likely the causes are still there and the C shape will get worse as you get older.

In fact, the worse it gets, the more of a role gravity will take in pushing it further out of shape. It's important that today you understand the way to fix it and you find time to do that every day if possible.

Note that, even if you do not yet have a visible C shape, you may well have the makings of one. The most common and debilitating of these Cs comes from a very common activity – sitting down.

In Chapter 3 we looked at how sitting on a chair and resting your back on the back rest can be so damaging to your posture. It is easy to see how a C position can develop, with the front of your body being the inside of the C and the back of it being the outside. This is the most worst kind of C position, as it affects virtually every part of the body, particularly the cardiovascular and digestive systems. Your heart, lungs and digestive organs are virtually collapsed in on themselves, and don't have the space or blood supply to function effectively.

As if all this wasn't bad enough, your legs hang down from the knees, shortening the hamstrings at the back of the legs and the hip flexors at the front. Often the feet hang down, thus shortening the calf muscles as well. Almost all the muscles that has developed over millennia to support you in a standing position are compromised.

If you spend a large part of each day sitting down, you will be affected. You will have tight hamstrings and hip flexors, abdominals, chest and SCM (sternocleidomastoid muscles, at the front of the neck). Your back muscles may not be strong enough to pull you upright.

I can't stress how important it is for people who spend a lot of their day sitting down to stretch regularly.

These stretches should include, as a minimum, the hamstrings, hip flexors and a back bend of some kind. The back bend should open up the whole front of the body, including the hip flexors, abdominals, chest and front of shoulders, all of which will have been compressed and contracted due to your inactivity in a seated position. You need to do this at least once a day to balance the damage that sitting does to your posture.

So many people choose to do stretches that feature almost exclusively front bends which do nothing to address the tightest areas of their body.

Stretch your own way

Each of us is unique in every way. Your genetic makeup, the way you've lived your life, the habitual way you deal with stress mean that you have your own unique patterns of tension in your muscles. Hence there is no use in comparing yourself, flexibility wise, to another person because no direct comparisons can be made. Take me as an example. I have relatively short legs and long arms, so it should be much easier for me to be able to touch my toes than someone with long legs and shorter arms. However, it's something I couldn't get anywhere near all through my school years until I took up kung fu shortly after leaving school, and regular practice finally made it possible. I often tell my students to ignore what the others are doing during stretches and focus on themselves. You are your only competition. Are you more flexible in this stretch than you were a couple of weeks ago?

Everyone will find certain stretches easy and others very hard. Obviously it's of limited use practising the easy ones. It is the hard stretches that point out where your tension patterns are and so those are where you should be focusing your energy and time. The rewards of increased flexibility are so great that it's well worth the few minutes once or twice a day that it takes. You should also try to vary not just which stretches you do but also how you do them, otherwise your routines will become just that: routine. This chapter has suggested a range of ways of varying your stretches such as using your breathing, passive movements, using core strength and stabilising in different ways.

How often should you stretch?

You should have realised by now that flexibility is a worthwhile goal to attain and that you should be putting aside a certain amount of time every day to increase your flexibility. Some days you may have more time available than on others, but even on the days when time is short you can still work on stretching three or four areas. At the very least you can do the two minute tension buster a few times. Bear in mind that all this can do is maintain the level of flexibility you have now. It won't improve it. So on days when you have more time, then you can work on more areas and on increasing your flexibility by working on softening your hard tension. Learn which are your problem areas and work more on those.

Many people – including me – find that first thing in the morning is a great time to stretch.

You should always find another two or three times during your day to do some very quick maintenance stretching. You will find that tension creeps back up on you very quickly, particularly if you've spent a reasonable amount of time in a fixed position on a chair. Get up, find some space, do those side, forward and back bends and also the dragon's back and snake's back exercises. Doing this in the middle of your day will enable you to feel which joints are still fairly flexible and which ones feel tight. This will tell you where you develop tension during your day, and will point to which maintenance stretches you need to do to keep yourself low on tension and high on energy as your day progresses. Just a few seconds of each of these maintenance stretches can, with practice, enable you to breeze through the soft tension that's built up and leave you feeling light, refreshed, free of tension and ready to face whatever your day may bring. You will feel a world better physically and mentally and will be far more productive afterwards.

Janet knew that her neck and shoulders particularly were carrying a lot of tension and were very immobile. She decided to make shoulder and neck mobility her priority, and spent a few minutes, three times a day, stretching them. She also did some more general stretches such as forward, backward and side bends. Like most people, she was amazed at how quickly tension crept back in again and realised that in order to keep it at bay properly she would have to stretch every hour, which was clearly impractical. Her shoulders started to respond to her increased mobility and the headaches that plagued her started to become less painful and occurred less often.

Peter knew that he had to work on releasing the huge tensions in the front of his body that were throwing his posture out of alignment. His abdomen, chest and front of shoulders were all working together to pull his trunk forwards. To start with, just lying on his back with no pillow

136

to support his head was a challenge. Gradually his 'front C' responded. Peter remembered that he also had to release the tension in his back, otherwise the muscles in his front would tighten up again to maintain the status quo. Peter spent 15 minutes twice a day stretching, and his mobility started to return. His posture also gradually changed for the better and this added to his new-found energy, as all his movements now seemed to be so much easier.

A summary of Chapter 8

A flexible body is one that has minimum tensions and so is able to easily cope with stresses. It makes you feel great and improves your posture and makes all movements much easier.

When stretching, move slowly and stabilise regularly while maintaining an imaginary pressure, and mentally open and release tensions. Then feel yourself being drawn further into the stretch.

Finally, and most importantly, stretch regularly. Occasional stretching is virtually useless; you should aim to stretch the important areas at least once a day.

CHAPTER 9

Touching your World

In this chapter

> I still find myself developing a lot of tension during my day.
> What could be the cause of this?

> I find it hard to relax and be comfortable in new surroundings.
> Can you help with this?

> I get nervous and contracted inside when approached by
> strangers or sometimes even people I know well. How can I
> combat this?

People who carry a lot of tension find it difficult to touch and be touched.
They are cut off from the people and things they care about, unable to truly
feel their bodies or the world around them, and are often clumsy in their
movements and gestures.

This chapter aims to change all that and to turn you into someone who is
more sensitive, graceful, better able to connect with others and has more
personal power and control.

In this chapter I will introduce you to the LIGHTER touch. This is an
acronym for the benefits you will gain when you learn to lighten your touch.
The acronym stands for:

Lighter
Intelligent
Graceful
Holistic
Tension-free
Echo
Responsive

LIGHTER touch

Throughout your life and particularly when under stress you, like everyone else, uses too much force in almost everything you do. A part of this is due to the build-up of tension in most of your muscles that has turned the use of excessive force into a set of habits that are hard to break.

When stressed, the situation becomes even worse. Without realising it, you grip your steering wheel tightly, slam doors, jab away at the keyboard and generally walk around with extra tension resisting every move you make. This 'bull in a china shop' approach wastes energy and contributes to the overall burden of tension you're carrying every day.

You should aim to use the minimum possible amount of force all the time. This requires mindfulness, which is in itself a major advantage. You can no longer rely on your habits to do anything because you will soon see that the habitual way you do virtually everything is inefficient. Learning to touch the world lightly will take some persistence and patience with yourself, but it really is worth it. Here's why...

Intelligent movement

When you start moving and handling objects more lightly, your brain has to work a little harder to find the most efficient way of achieving its task. Whereas before brute strength may have worked in some circumstances, now you must learn to become more observant and more intelligent in your movements.

As a simple example, we keep clothes drying racks in our cupboard under the stairs. Sometimes they get tangled with each other or the vacuum cleaner, ironing board etc. Instead of just forcing them out and then having to put everything back in again, it is more efficient and less irritating to see where they're tangled and gently disentangle them.

In Jade Dragon kung fu, we are constantly analysing our own and our opponent's position to see how best to position the body to be able to absorb or redirect an attack with the most efficiency. It is at least as much about brain power as it is about physical ability.

Graceful Power

In tai chi chuan (very much a Daoist art), you learn to move the body in a graceful and balanced way. Every movement is expressed using the whole body; there are no localised movements. If you are extending an arm it is not just the arm and shoulder muscles involved, but also the legs, hips, back and so on. This global balancing of every movement makes everything strong and effortless. It also means that tension is far less likely to build up in local muscles, as the force is spread throughout the body.

When a normal person reaches out and meets resistance in the shape of an object, such as a wall or a door, the tendency is for local muscles in the arm and shoulder to push against the resistance briefly. A person trained in the Daoist movement arts such as tai chi chuan will react differently. As their weight is sunk into the ground and the arm movement is supported by the overall physical structure they will feel the resistance through their whole body down through their feet into the ground. Their body absorbs the shock and directs it downwards, no matter how hard or soft the contact.

Lack of tension dramatically increases your sensitivity and speed of reflexes.

Through this kind of training, the practitioner learns to use the core, postural muscles to stabilise the body and gentle contractions of the mobilising muscles to move it. The movements come from the core of the body – the legs generate the power, which moves the centre of the body which, in turn, moves the arms and trunk. This is in stark contrast to the majority of people who move the arms or head first and the rest of the body follows.

Holistic actions

This grace or lack of tension results in movements that are holistic. In other words, each movement uses as much of the body as possible. In higher levels the body, mind and breath act as one unit so that you are putting all of yourself into everything you do. Most people are scattered; their arms and legs do their own thing disconnected from each other, the breath is uncontrolled, simply keeping pace with oxygen and CO_2 requirements, and the mind is somewhere else entirely – usually reliving the past or worrying about the future. Because most people are so disconnected, they are living their lives in a small part of themselves and as a result they feel small compared to the people and circumstances around them. Problems seem big because they feel small and powerless.

When you learn to move and live holistically you will feel, and become, much more powerful and your problems will shrink in comparison. Every action will become more focused and you will become more decisive and assertive.

Tension-free

When you apply too much force to any movement, tension begins to back up like cars in a traffic jam. Let's try a little experiment. I want you to clench one of your hands into a fist as tightly as you can and hold it for about five seconds. To close the fingers and thumb in tightly towards the palm of the hand requires tension in the muscles of the forearm. However, I bet you also tensed muscles in your arms, shoulders and possibly neck, back and chest as well. Try it again, and you'll see. None of the tension in those other areas will add to the strength of the grip, but because they are also tensed it just feels stronger.

Now try to clench your hands into fists without tensing your arms, shoulders or anywhere else. This is more difficult, but is an extremely useful exercise. You must really focus on the areas you want to stay relaxed to ensure they don't start tensing up without your knowledge. This is a key exercise that I teach in my kung fu class. It means that the practitioner is able to clench a fist or grab a hold of a person without tensing their arms and shoulders. By doing so, they are able to react very quickly to whatever movement their opponent makes. Any excess tension would slow down and weaken their reaction as well as drain them of energy.

Why is this exercise so important? Simply because it helps you to learn to use your hands without tensing your arms and shoulders. I'm sure many of you drive a car. If you do, I'm sure you have experienced times when your hands were gripped tightly on the steering wheel and that tension crept up your arms into your shoulders, back and chest. This is what can cause fatigue, headaches and eyestrain on long journeys. Or perhaps you have been writing and found that you were gripping then pen so hard that the tension had crept up and overtaken your upper body (exams are terrible for this). Any action you take with your hands that involves gripping runs the risk of that gripping tension spreading and causing you short- or long- term misery or pain. Try this now: even gripping something lightly often involves a slight tensing of the bicep simply as an habitual response. The more aware you are of your movements and habits, the faster you can rid yourself of them.

Echoing feedback

When I say 'echo' I am referring to the sensual feedback you get from lightly touching a person or object. When you press something hard, the only feedback you tend to get is the increased tension in your muscles from applying the pressure. Touch something softly, though, and your sensitive fingertips will convey much more data about the object to your brain.

When you stroke something softly you can feel its texture and its temperature, and I believe the reason for this is related to the previous section. When you touch something softly you aren't generating a lot of unnecessary tension which then blocks or impedes the neural pathways getting to the brain. As a result, the impressions you get are stronger and the brain has more to work with in analysing the sensory data.

Visually impaired people need to rely more on their sense of touch, and so they need to stay focused, relaxed and in the moment in order to pick up the sensory and audio cues in their environment.

We all use our sense of touch all the time. Walking would be almost impossible without it, eating would be a major struggle, writing or typing would be far harder.

Spend a few moments now focusing on all the touch sensations you can. The way your clothes touch your body, the feelings in your fingers and hands and feet, the way your lips are pressed together, the feeling of the seat under you and so on. Just concentrating on these things can release tension and help you to stay focused in the here and now.

Value your sense of touch and use only as much force as is necessary in the way you touch your world.

Responsive reactions

This is related to the above point. The more feedback you can get from your sense of touch, then the faster and more accurate will be your response. Take typing as an example. If, like me, you can touch–type, try banging each key hard and see what that does to your typing speed and accuracy. I just tried that while typing the last sentence, and didn't get a single word correct. Any movement you do regularly should by now be fairly refined and won't lead to too much excess tension. However, new moves and new skills are a different matter. Often we subconsciously tense more muscles than necessary, which makes learning the new skill much harder.

Since many movements involve many muscles spread throughout the body, any tension anywhere can slow down reaction times throughout the body. A good example of this is walking on ice or snow. A general tendency is to stiffen up, just in case you fall but, in doing so, you are decreasing your ability to react quickly should you lose your balance and so you are making yourself much more likely to fall over. A much better strategy is to use the 'walk of awareness' which keeps the head over the centre line, maintains balance and helps you to relax downwards through your feet and into the ground. You will be more stable and balanced and better able to make the small changes to your alignment necessary if you feel you are losing your balance. Indeed, overcompensating is probably one of the biggest faults people make when they start to lose their balance. Their arms and legs windmill wildly and they have little idea of precisely how to bring their body back into alignment with gravity. The more you can practise perfect alignment, the easier it will be for you to keep it.

The main point here is that a lighter touch means less tension, which leads to faster reactions when you need them.

Here are two other points that I couldn't fit into the LIGHTER acronym.

Energy, conservation of

Using too much force in everything you do wears you out faster: it's as simple as that. Energy is like money in the bank. If you want more of it, then you need to either earn more or spend less. Most things you do in life are costing you more in energy terms than you need to spend.

Respect and reverence

When you hold an object with a light touch it shows more respect, even reverence, for the object. You will become far more aware of the qualities of the object, its weight, shape and feel. By paying more attention to it you will appreciate it more – this is a very useful lesson for children to learn who tend to abuse toys and then lose or forget them.

In fact, it seems to be an ingrained habit in most of us to treat the things we value with respect by holding them gently. Many things that are intrinsically valuable are also fragile and so require a light touch. Unfortunately, I believe we are losing this respect. Most products now are not meant to be looked after but to be used for a while and then thrown away and replaced by a newer model. There is no longer the culture of looking after objects lest they need to be taken away and repaired. As a result of this, the way many people treat valuable objects is terrible. I have no particular attachment to material objects but I do recognise that a lack of respect for things also means a lack of respect for other people.

Learn to value the things you have and treat them gently, if for no other reason than they will last longer!

Feel the weight

When lifting any object, no matter what its size or weight, hold it gently and feel its weight as you lift it. Feel how that weight generates compensatory tension in different parts of your body. Feel how moving the object around changes some of the tension and the route it takes through you. Remember that the less tension you are carrying the more feedback you will have.

This is how the great swordsmen of old learned to become one with their weapon. The allowed the feeling of the blade to flow through their whole body instead of just using their hand and arm.

It is this kind of exercise that will enable you to improve your strength. If you are used to just using your arm muscles to lift objects and little else, then you are severely limiting your potential. You should be aiming to use the bigger muscles of your legs, hips and trunk, and leaving the tension out of the arms as much as possible. In doing so, you are making the task easier and allowing a huge reserve of muscle power for when you really need it.

Always be comfortable

You cannot easily relax without being comfortable and,
likewise, you cannot be comfortable if you aren't relaxed.

Be comfortable wherever you find yourself and give in to your surroundings. Always try to avoid internally resisting what is happening to you, as that only develops tension and internal blockages.

You can do this by simply imagining that whatever you are touching is soft, warm and comfortable. Allow yourself to relax into it.

This simple practice can have remarkable effects. Instead of internally fighting against your environment, just accept it as it is and act as if it is the most comfortable place in the world. So even if it is pouring with rain and freezing cold do not allow this to cause you to contract internally. Smile, expand outwards through your five peripheral points and stay open and relaxed.

Touching your world in practice

Your aim, of course, is to gradually change your habitual ways of performing everyday actions so as to use less tension. This, however, is not going to happen overnight. You will need to consciously carry out your everyday tasks until the act of maintaining some conscious attention on what you're doing has, in itself, become a habit.

This is no easy task and the best way is to choose just one activity, do it consciously and strive to apply the principle of lightness of touch. Whether it be driving to work, vacuuming the house or making the evening meal try to be aware, as much as possible, of precisely what you are doing and how you are doing it. This becomes a form of moving meditation and is very good for the mind as well as the body. When you first start doing this, you may be amazed at how much unnecessary force you have been using up until now. Try to apply as many of the principles in this book as you can. Get your posture right, breathe into and move from your centre, and try to use your centre to carry each movement as much as you can. Now that you are no longer tied to your old habitual ways of doing things, you can experiment with different movements and muscles. Remember that it is your old habits that have locked you into the patterns of tension that you're carrying around. Change those habits into healthier ones, otherwise any release of tension that you earn will still be fighting against your old, tension-inducing habits.

This is a journey of self-discovery and will give you a genuine opportunity to reinvent yourself and the way you react to your world.

Here are a few tips:

When driving: Hold the steering wheel lightly with your fingers. Keep your elbows weighted downwards to prevent your shoulders from rising. Where possible, steer by focusing on moving your hands from the elbows; don't focus on the hands. This will keep your grip light. When changing gear, hold the gearstick lightly and, again, move it from your elbow, not your hand.

When using a computer keyboard: Keep your elbows relaxed downwards and your hands hovering over the keys. Be aware of your seated position – use your postural muscles to keep you upright, not the back of your chair.

When doing household chores: Remember the principles of posture and effortless movement – keep your weight low, move from your centre, relax your elbows downwards and use only the minimum force necessary. Even the most mundane of tasks can become a way of challenging and developing yourself to attain a new level of mastery!

Touching others

Some people are very touchy-feely. Others recoil at the touch of another person. Everyone also has their own personal space requirements, and these can vary drastically from person to person.

Your personal space refers to the amount of distance between yourself and another person that you find comfortable. When another person gets too close, it makes you feel uncomfortable and instinctively you will contract inwards to protect yourself.

The amount of personal space you need varies depending on your relationship to the other person, the circumstances and what you have grown up with and been used to. Generally speaking, the better you know someone then the closer you will allow them to get. Obviously, you would allow a lover to get much closer to you than your creepy boss! Circumstances also play a part – in a crowded lift or bar, you have no choice but to allow your personal space to be violated. Most people react to this by contracting inwards, showing no expression or emotion and avoiding eye contact with others.

There are always going to be occasions when you feel that your personal space is being violated. This may be accidental, such as on a crowded tube, or on purpose, by somebody trying to control you, such as an abusive spouse or boss. When this happens, remember that contracting inwards is a habit. Feel it happening and consciously combat it by expanding outwards into your five peripheral points. Straightaway this will make you feel more relaxed, much stronger and more in control of yourself and the situation.

Always remember that the more you practise these skills the better they will work for you. You need to get to a point where nobody and no situation can make you respond in a negative way.

By being more in control of yourself, you are better able to control the situation that is threatening your safety and internal stability.

Physical touch is an enormously powerful thing. A touch can express so much – support, love, playfulness, rejection or anger. Many people, particularly those who have been violently or sexually abused in the past, try to avoid another person's touch at all costs. They will have large personal space bubbles and can feel violated by any physical display. Touch can be an important part of the way you communicate with others, but you must be aware of how the other person reacts. Before you can touch someone, you must get through their personal bubble. As you do so are they pulling away, tensing up or showing any other signs of discomfort? You are learning to become much more aware of yourself, so now you need to become equally aware of the feelings of others. Respect their personal space and be aware that you can touch them with a word or with a look, which can be just as expressive as a physical touch.

Many other people crave physical affection, but in our touch-phobic culture rarely get any. They feel valued, validated and energised from physical touch. Again, being aware of the feelings and body language of others enables you to see people who are like this and will enable you to connect with them more deeply. As you go through their personal space they will open up to you, even reach out. It may be with an open arm or a smaller hand gesture, but if you care for them the message is clear. They want you to show how much you care by the act of touching. In our culture we are so wary of accusations of sexual abuse that the natural and human act of touching another is becoming increasingly unsocial, even criminalised. My five year old daughter is forbidden to hug or kiss her playmates in school, and I find that such a sad thing.

I firmly believe that the less contracted and tense you are, then the better you are able to touch the world and the people around you. You become more graceful, waste less effort and are better able to empathise with others – which is one of the most important communication skills. In short, everything you do becomes easier and more efficient.

Being at home
Finally, here is a simple trick to help you feel comfortable in any strange place you may find yourself.

Many people feel uncomfortable in new surroundings. Whether it be a party or a job interview, the act of walking into a strange place that everyone around you seems to already know can make you feel uncomfortable. The answer, yet again, can be found in expanding. This time imagine yourself, your aura and your energy expanding to fill the whole room and everyone and everything in it. You are the whole room, and this will make you feel big, powerful and also comfortable that you are safe in an area that is a part of you. I'm sure you know someone who can walk into any room and act as if they own it – you may have secretly envied them their confidence. Now it can be yours too.

A summary of Chapter 9

Excess tension causes you to use too much force in everything you do. By lightening your touch you hold on to less tension, conserve energy, perform tasks with more efficiency and balance and are able to respond more quickly and appropriately when your situation changes.

As well as becoming more aware of yourself, you can also become more aware of your effects on others and your immediate environment. Quickly you begin to realise that changing the way you do things can make tasks much easier, and that being more comfortable in your own skin makes people around you more comfortable.

Everyone has a personal space bubble. You may feel threatened when yours is invaded and contract in on yourself. Learn to consciously expand out to your peripheral points to release that tension and regain control of your body. You can then further expand out to fill the whole room with your mind and energy. In this way you will feel comfortable, confident and at home wherever you may find yourself.

CHAPTER 10

The Quest for Happiness

In this chapter

> Why aren't we just automatically happy? Why does it seem to be so beyond the reach of most people simply to be content?
>
> Surely happiness means different things to different people. How can I know what areas of my life to focus on that will make me happier?
>
> Sometimes I can't believe how life is treating me, and it makes me really angry. I can feel the tension rising inside me. Can I inoculate myself against that?

Happiness is a difficult concept to define. Again, dictionaries try their best but happiness means such different things to different people. If we all had the same concept of happiness then it would be easier for us to know how to achieve it.

What does the word 'happiness' mean to you? For some people it's having enough money to live in comfort and luxury for the rest of their life. For others it's finding true love; while for others it could be escaping from the rat race and doing something meaningful with their lives.

> *Happiness comes not from having what you want but from wanting what you have.*

There is a great truth in this old saying. So many people rush through life just focused on achieving the next milestone or in buying the next item on their life's shopping list. But when they have that item they only appreciate it for a very short time before focusing on the next thing. That initial focus on attaining it soon fades away and the item or position or partner etc soon gets taken for granted.

Take a few moments now to reflect on the things you have in your life: home, job, partner, family , car, possessions, friendships etc. See them as if for the first time and appreciate them in the same way you did when they first came into your life. I often spend time looking around the house or at my wife and children and I feel so lucky and blessed to have them. So when things aren't going your way it really helps to stop and truly appreciate the things that are in your life and are really working for you.

The ten paths to happiness

Having said that happiness is a state of mind and there is no single cause for it, just as there is no one single cause for anger or depression. In this chapter I have listed ten paths to happiness. Using this list, you can score yourself on each of these paths and this will show you which aspects of your life are fulfilling and which aspects may be holding you back. Some of these paths will be much more important to you than others and, indeed, some are things you can't change easily. So if you feel you are being made miserable by things you can't change, then look at the list at what you *can* change and work on those. You may well find that other areas start to improve as well. The first three are things that everybody can work on, and are the subject of this book. Remember that you don't need to score highly on all of them to be happy. Some people can be very happy, despite lacking money or control over their destiny. They are happy because they score highly in other areas. Read through the list and descriptions below, score yourself out of ten for each area and add up your total. This would be a good exercise to do at the beginning of every year to see how your life has changed during the previous twelve months.

The ten paths are as follows:

1. Free yourself from stress and tension.

2. Work on achieving good physical and mental health.

3. Gain a strong sense of self-identity.

4. Work on being in control of your destiny.

5. Gain financial freedom.

6. Belong to a group/family/community/religion.

7. Be in a fulfilling relationship.

8. Have a path or goal to follow in life that you find fulfilling.

9. Think positively – see the good in what you have and also the good in others.

10. Make life better for others.

1. Free yourself from stress and tension

If you have read through this book so far and tried some of the exercises, you will already have felt some of their effects. You may already have discovered that your newly reduced tension levels mean that some of the things that used to make you angry or anxious or depressed no longer have such an effect on you. You are more in control of yourself and the ways in which you react to the stresses in your life. This, in itself, is a big first step towards being happier. Suffice to say, the less tension you are carrying around with you, the easier everything in your life will become. You will have far more energy and, for me, energy and happiness are almost synonymous.

When your body can move and express itself freely and easily, it is as if a weight has been lifted off your mind. Self-expression, particularly through any kind of movement, is an enormously powerful thing. That is why dance has always been so popular.

2. Work on achieving good physical and mental health

Your physical and mental/emotional health are affected to a very large degree by your tension levels. You now know this to be true, but lack of tension isn't the be-all and end-all of good health. You may have medical conditions that aren't related to your tensions at all. Clearly, if these are affecting your quality of life then they will affect your happiness levels. It is possible to be even terminally ill and still be happy if you score highly on most of the other criteria. If you have led a fulfilling life that has enriched you and others, if you are surrounded by a loving family and have maintained a positive outlook, if you have a faith that life doesn't end just because your physical shell dies then you can remain happy until your last breath.

I am a firm believer that you need to take responsibility for your own health and your own life. You need to take steps every day to keep yourself well. Don't regularly abuse your body and then expect medical science to patch you up. Medical science is great for when you have been unexpectedly injured or have been infected by a pathogen. Unfortunately, too many of the resources of our hospitals and doctors are being spent on patching up people whose lifestyles have led to their illnesses. That isn't a path to happiness.

3. Gain a strong sense of self-identity

This may be the most important of all. Many people believe that they don't matter. They think they're small and unimportant and so they feel at the mercy of fate, circumstance and anyone who wants to take advantage of them. When bad things happen to them they lack the resources to cope. They are disconnected from themselves and the world around them. The exercises in this book, particularly the rooting yourself to the ground and the breathing exercises, will all work to strengthen your sense of self. Gradually, all the parts of you will work together harmoniously and this will give you the strength to become larger than your problems. When this happens, then happiness will no longer be something that can only happen to others.

The stronger your sense of who you are, then the happier you are capable of being.

4. Work on being in control of your destiny

Even if you aren't in the corporate rat race, everyone has things that they are forced to do every day. Whether it's the monotony of a dull job (and I've had more than my fair share of those) or the daily grind of shopping, washing, cleaning and ironing, monotony can easily turn to misery. Just as bad is the constant stresses of high-pressure corporate careers. It's often not just the work itself but the office politics that can be hugely stressful.

What people with monotonous, routine jobs and corporate high-fliers have in common is a lack of control over their destinies. It manifests itself in different ways, but the effect is the same. Someone with a routine job is a very small cog in a very big system that they're unable to change. They have to fit into the machine and the machine allows little, if any, self-expression. The corporate man or woman lives in a world of targets and turmoil. Constantly under pressure to perform better than those around them, they often feel that the treadmill is getting faster and faster and if they make one small slip they could fall off. Underperform and you run the risk of losing your position but perform too well and you run the risk of causing jealousy and insecurity in your colleagues or boss and somehow being stabbed in the back. The stresses build up, and tensions inside you build up until they cause either physical health problems or mental breakdown. Neither the human body or the human mind is designed for such stress.

5. Gain financial freedom

For many people, having financial freedom is akin to happiness. Unfortunately, as all too many lottery winners would attest, money doesn't always buy you happiness. Money can certainly take away many of the stresses of life and provide security – assuming, of course, that you don't blow it all on material excesses. Personally, I would follow the old Chinese adage of spending a third or keeping it in cash, putting the second third in property and the final third in business or shares. That way, you are putting your money to work for you and sensibly limiting the amount that you have available to spend.

Money is important in life and it can also give you control over your destiny but in itself it won't guarantee happiness.

6. Belong to a group/family/community/religion

A sense of belonging seems to be an important aspect of happiness. Humans are social creatures and feel the need to belong to something larger than themselves. Families have always played a crucial role in happiness. A mutually supportive family provides support and stability through good times and bad. Becoming more community-minded can help you to feel a greater sense of belonging to the place you live. One of the attractions of religion is that sense of belonging to a worldwide group of people with the same beliefs as you.

One of the only problems with this is the sense of loss you feel if you ever have to leave the group. Many people rely on their group for stability and energy. In fact, some of the most devastating experiences come from no longer belonging to a group. This includes being disowned by your parents, being excommunicated from your church, sacked from your job and so on.

The group that once nourished you no longer wants you – and that can be terrifying.

Indeed, some people only seem to come alive in the right company. It's as if they have a dimmer switch inside them that is usually set to dim but in the right group it is turned up to full brightness. You need to be able to turn up your own dimmer switch and let its brightness flood you with energy and dazzle those around you. This strong inner self will see you through all the hardships and trials in your life. Happiness doesn't come from a life without problems but from the knowledge that you have the internal strength and resources to deal with the slings and arrows of outrageous fortune.

7. Be in a fulfilling relationship

This has much the same effect as being in a group. A good relationship can help you affirm who you are, can nourish you and provide emotional stability. For this to happen, it is vital that neither party does anything that could belittle the other. I always find it shocking when I see couples arguing and saying anything they can to hurt their partner and put them down. What is really needed in situations like this is to see the other person's point of view. In fact, more than that – what is needed is to try to feel what they are feeling, to open up to their experiences and emotions so that you can fully empathise with them. If you can both do that, then conflict will no longer exist. So for those of you who have a partner, cherish them and help them to become more than they are through your words and actions. Remember that we each behave as we are treated. If someone treats you like an idiot, then that is how you will start behaving. But treat someone as if they were the most wonderful, vibrant and loving person in the world, and they will start to become that person.

For those of you who are looking for a life partner, never stop believing that they will come. When the time is right, when you are at the right stage in your life's journey, then the right person will come along. Follow the guidelines above and cherish that person and maintain empathy with them through the good times and bad that will lie ahead.

Finally, remember that nothing lasts forever, not even beautiful relationships. This is why I continue to remind you that having a strong sense of self is so vital. It alone can sustain you at those times when nothing and nobody else can. It may seem strange for me to tell you that good breathing and postural habits can help you through relationship break-ups, but they are more powerful than you may think. It is your self-control and your ability to change the way you react to life's changes (and disasters) that you need to keep working on.

8. Have a path to follow in life that you find fulfilling

If you talk to anyone who has found any measure of success or happiness in their life, then you will often find that they have followed a path to get there. The path may be one that they created or one that they have followed that was set by another but, either way, it has been their guiding beacon.

Going through life without a path to follow is like going out for a drive with no idea of where you're going. Eventually you may get somewhere interesting – but you might not. Even if you do, it will take a long time to get there. For those who are following a map or know in their heads where they're going, then they may travel there via different routes but they will get there. There may be traffic jams or road closures along the way but they will not give up; instead, they will find another route to their destination and they will get there.

9. Think positively – see the good in what you have and also the good in others

We all know, or think we know, that happiness is just around the corner. When I get that pay rise I'll be happy, if I can get that person to go on a date with me I'll be happy, if I can lose those 12 pounds I'll be happy. We all think these kind of thoughts and truly believe that if circumstances were just slightly different then happiness would come. But would it? Where is the evidence for this?

"People are just as happy as they make up their minds to be." Abraham Lincoln

The trouble is, we all want things but then when we get them the joy soon wears off and we start to feel we can't be happy until we get the next thing. Happiness will always, then, lie just around the corner until you turn that corner and realise that there's yet another corner to go.

There is not a single material thing on this planet that will make you happy in the long term.

The only time and place you can be happy is right here and right now. Look around you and appreciate, deeply appreciate, everything you see. There is so much in life that is beautiful yet goes unnoticed because you are too wrapped up in your own personal dramas. All of your life, all your achievements, all your choices have led up to this point. It's easy to be negative about yourself and your life but remember that every life has its stresses, its responsibilities, its repetitiveness. You could be rich and famous and still find life intolerably stressful with masses of responsibility and times of interminable tedium. Why do you think so many celebrities turn to drugs? Real happiness lies in appreciating what you've got and what you've achieved. Look around at your possessions and recall the pleasure you got when you first acquired them. Look at your friends and family, and remember the wonderful times you've had with them. Look around and really see your environment. It is a part of you as much as you are a part of it.

10. Make life better for others

Giving to others is a natural human pleasure. Part of the fun of Christmas lies in giving gifts to others, to consider what they'd really like and anticipate the look on their face when they open that special gift.

Many people choose, or wish they had chosen, a career that involves helping others. Whether nursing or aid work, dedicating your life to easing the suffering of others gives your life some meaning. But even if your job doesn't involve making life better for others, there are plenty of ways in which you can still give your time and/or money to help. I know that many readers may be thinking that they don't have enough time and no spare money and, although they'd love to help, they aren't able to at the moment. I can completely understand this attitude – I've been there many times myself. However, we are living in an age when more and more people have less and less, and this is unlikely to change in the foreseeable future. There are thousands of charities which do great work and always need people to donate their money or time. It is often more rewarding to give your time than your money. This is not wasted time; far from it. On your deathbed you will remember the hours you gave to charity and you'll be glad and proud that you did.

Having read through the ten points above, give yourself a score out of ten for each. Your total will tell you how happy you are as a percentage of how happy you could be. Happiness doesn't mean you have to score highly on each of them, but if you score low on all of them then it's unlikely that happiness will come easily to you. This list is enormously useful. You may feel that you can't be happy until you have a loving partner or a better job – but this list will show you other ways to make your life better.

Many people feel that happiness comes from certainty. With change comes stress which leads to resistance which leads to tension and misery. But change can sometimes be positive and can lead to the happiest times we've ever had. Think about the times in your life when you've felt true joy. An exciting holiday, a new romance, a challenging new job and so on. But we often find that life is capricious and that change is inevitable – is your new romantic interest really interested in you; will your new job be all you hoped or is it just a more sexed up version of the same old rat race and so on. Soon the excess energy of happiness drains away and you start to expect to see cracks in the glossiness of what could have been.

Don't let this happen to you.

I am a firm believer that the more you expect bad things to happen to you then the more bad things will happen to you. You don't need me to provide evidence for this — we all know that people who expect the worst get the worst. So this next idea may seem radical and even, perhaps, impossible to achieve but here it is:

Make happiness your default state.

In the wonderful book "The Way of the Peaceful Warrior" by Dan Millman he describes the pursuit of 'unreasonable happiness'. That is being happy even when it seems unreasonable to be so. This is precisely what I mean. Why shouldn't you be happy right now. All you need do is act as if you were full of joy and your body and mind will work together to create the same feelings, energy, chemicals etc that you would produce if you were happy due to some

159

external event such as an upcoming holiday. It's just like the placebo effect which can produce physical changes due to your belief in a cure. Instead of leaving your wellbeing in the hands of fate, take control of your emotional state right now and decide to be happy. Your external circumstances don't matter one jot – that is what makes it unreasonable but there is nothing else on earth that can give you the same high level of energy and wellbeing than the feeling of joy and happiness. No matter what is going on in your life right now treat yourself to feeling happy and keep doing it often enough to make it a habit. Your new-found enjoyment of life will soon start to affect the people and situations around you and life will start going your way again. This really does work.

The roots of misery

We have discussed the ten criteria for happiness and decided that leaving your happiness to fate is short-changing you. I'm sure you can see the benefits on focusing on the areas of your life which you can change and just taking the decision to be happy anyway whatever happens. However, there will still be times when misery will rear its ugly head and demand entrance into your life. Where does it come from?

Misery largely comes from resistance to what is. When something that you perceive as bad happens to you, then you resist physically and mentally. Physical resistance comes in the form of tension while mental resistance comes to you as misery.

When something bad happens to you, you spend a period of time – which could vary from seconds to the rest of your life – refusing to believe it's true. You gnash your teeth, bemoan and bewail your lot. In short, you become angry or depressed or – if it's something you can't deal with – you bury it deep inside you under layers of protective tension.

Bad things will happen to you, but the sooner you are able to accept the change in your circumstances then the sooner you will be able to adapt and move on.

It is the people who aren't able to accept change and refuse to adapt to it who suffer in life. Daoism teaches us that life continues to move onwards whether you're stuck in the past or not. Life is like a great river carrying us along in its flow. Sometimes you will bump into obstacles in your path. You can either grab hold of them and keep hold of them so that you never forget the pain they caused you – or let go of them and continue along the flow of your life. How many traumas in your past are you refusing to let go of, and how are they holding you back in your life? It can take some serious introspection to find and resolve your old blockages but it is time well worth spending.

Ultimately, though, your happiness should not depend on anything but should be your default state of mind. Although I have listed ten criteria, each of which can affect your outward happiness, in time you can achieve constant happiness under almost any conditions. Always remember that happiness is never around the corner because around the corner doesn't exist and may never do. The only time that exists is now, so the only time it is possible for you to be happy is right now.

There is another powerful principle called 'acting as if'. To take an extreme example, if you wanted to be a ballet dancer you should act as if you already were one. You would eat what they do, exercise like they do, discipline yourself like they do and so on. Gradually you would become just like a bona fide ballet dancer. It is the same with happiness. Act right now as if you are the happiest person in the world. Smile, feel the energy grow inside you and overflow into your movements. Let it show on your face and affect the world around you. Here is an exercise that will help you smile through life and use your smile to open up your tensions and protect you from day-to-day stresses.

The whole-body smile

This is a lovely exercise that uses the power of a smile to fill your whole body with happiness and energy. You should learn to wear your whole-body smile like you do your clothes. Put it on when you get up in the morning, and keep it on all day. It may sound like it can take a while but with a little practice you can go through the whole procedure in just a few seconds.

1. Smile with your mouth, feel it grow and extend it up into your eyes. Your eyes will take that happy movement of the mouth and boost

it around the rest of your body and outwards towards everyone you meet.

2. Let the smile fill and open up your whole face, particularly around the mouth and jaw.

3. Feel the smile in the tight muscles of your neck. Let it linger there for a while, opening up and energising this vital area.

4. Drop your smile down into your chest. Open up the muscles of your chest and upper back. Smile directly into your heart and lungs. See if you can feel their movement in your chest.

5. Lower the smile into your abdomen and lower back. Open up this chronically tight area. Breathe into it and combine the smile and breath to bring light and power into your centre.

6. Smile into your hips and groin area. As always, use your mind to try and feel inside yourself. Whatever you can feel, then energise with your smile.

7. Smile all the way down through your legs and into your feet. Then all the way down through your arms and into your hands.

8. Feel the smile everywhere inside you. Feel it grow and grow until it radiates outwards into your surroundings. The brighter it glows, the more stresses it will be able to protect you against. Soon you will be almost impervious to the effects of fear and stress. You will be able to feel which parts of yourself lose their inner smile and can focus on re-energising them.

Your whole-body smile will send positive signals down through your body, helping you to accept yourself as you are. This will help you to open up and release many deep tensions. This is the real power of this exercise. All too often, the signals we send ourselves are critical and these negative signals serve only to close our bodies up and cut ourselves off from our minds. It's important that you overwhelm those negative thought patterns with the positive energy of your whole-body smile.

Peter was enjoying his increased mastery over his breathing, posture and stress levels. He could now focus on his life and his future. He realised that he had been identifying too much with his last job, and losing it was like losing his identity. He started to make contact with his friends again and he also spent more time outdoors pursuing his hobbies of enjoying nature and photography. He started to be called for more interviews and he knew that his increased self-confidence and better posture would stand him in good stead.

Janet realised that her high-pressure job was having a negative effect on her health and sanity. She went on holiday with her partner to give herself some breathing space to consider her options. Through learning to breathe out her troubles and connect more solidly to the earth, she was bringing her stress and panic under control. She now felt more assertive and in control of her life and so opened up to her partner about how she felt about her job. He confirmed that he had been worried about her stress levels, although felt that they seemed to be more under control now. Janet is now deciding whether her high salary is worth the endless pressure, even though she now seems able to deal with it more effectively. She will continue to work on her posture, flexibility and breathing and during her holiday she started the 'whole-body smile'. All of a sudden, her problems seem so much smaller. She can deal with this; all it takes is a meeting with her manager. She will leave the rest to fate.

I hope you have enjoyed this book. There are a lot of principles and practices contained here. They all work, but I don't expect you to try them all at once. Try a few of them out and try to make them a part of your life for a week or two and see how your life changes. If any of them don't work for you, then there are plenty of other practices in here that may work better for your particular personality, circumstances and tension patterns. This book has been written for you to return to again and again, and each time will bring new insights and practices to help you live a life freer of tension and with more vitality and vigour. Your aim should be to hardwire these principles and practices into your body and your life. The way you habitually react to change itself will start to change. Indeed, the way you react to those changes will define who you are. Some of you may consider this to be too much like hard work and will give up easily. However, I hope that most of you will make the few changes necessary to reap some of the benefits. When things start changing for the better for you, it will motivate you to apply more of the principles in this book.

And finally...

Finally, if I had to put all the stuff in this book into a few simple principles, they would read as follows:

> Become more aware of yourself and your tensions, learn to soften and expand them and drop them downwards. Connect to the ground to give you personal power.

> Become aware of your centre, breathe into it and expand from there outwards through your whole body and outwards into your immediate environment. Let what is outside you become a part of you.

> Develop flexibility of body and mind, and don't let a day go by when you don't seek to develop that.

> Touch the world lightly, conserve your energy and keep your power inside.

> Smile and let your smile slowly flow through and flood your whole body. Let nothing dim the brightness of your whole-body smile.

INDEX

ABOUT THE AUTHOR

Paul Chapman is a kung fu and tai chi master, an author and a stress coach. He has a huge range of knowledge on health, fitness, internal development, martial arts, psychology and spirituality. Since 2003 he has run the Jade Dragon Kung Fu School in England.

He is a firm believer that it is tension and not stress that is the cause of many of our ills. He is an inspiring and generous teacher, full of stories and amazing demonstrations who has helped hundreds of individuals to release their tensions and unlock their potential. "Stress Proof Your Body" is his first book but he aims to write many more.

Paul has spent most of his adult life in the fields of human health, fitness and potential. He has qualifications in fields as diverse as weight training, sports therapy and hypnotherapy. He has run fitness centres and lectured at college level in Sports Science, Biomechanics and Psychology.

For more information see his websites:
For stress coaching - yourstresscoach.co.uk
For kung fu and tai chi training – jadedragonschool.com

Paul Chapman lives near Reading, England.

Made in the USA
Monee, IL
13 October 2022

15799403R00104